Birds of New Jersey

To my mother and father,
    with thanks for wonderful hours afield,
and to my wife, Mary,
    who now shares the outdoor trails

BIRDS OF
NEW JERSEY

Their Habits and Habitats

Charles Leck

RUTGERS UNIVERSITY PRESS

New Brunswick, New Jersey

Library of Congress Cataloging in Publication Data

Leck, Charles, 1944–
    Birds of New Jersey, their habits and habitats.

    Bibliography: p.
    1. Birds—New Jersey. I. Title.
QL684.N5L4   598.2′9749   75-2112

FIRST PAPERBACK PRINTING, WITH CORRECTIONS

Contents

List of Illustrations

Maps

List of Tables

Page

Preface

New Jersey has a rich diversity of birds from a wide variety of natural communities. It has large areas of ocean, beach, pine forest, deciduous forest, salt marsh, fields, and scattered fresh-water marshes, ponds, lakes, bogs, and mountain ridges. At least fifty per cent of the State is still in a fairly natural condition, though the population is highly urbanized (one third of New Jerseyans live on five per cent of the land), and agricultural uses are actually declining. At the same time the State has progressively allocated tracts as natural areas for preservation.

The birdlife of New Jersey has been studied since the visits of John James Audubon in 1832. Because ornithology began so early in New Jersey and because the State has a greater density of bird watchers than any other state, New Jersey ranks high in the number of known bird species, with 410 recorded. Any person who actively enjoys bird-watching can easily find more than 200 species in New Jersey in any year. Further, the State benefits from its geographic position on the Atlantic Flyway—New Jersey is probably the best location on the eastern coast to observe the great fall migrations.

This book is intended to provide an introduction to the avifauna of the State. It is a companion to one's field guide and is not an identification manual but a complementary review of New Jersey bird communities and bird-watching. There will be changes in the future, particularly with man's

alteration of the environment. But with appropriate priori-
ties New Jersey may continue to be graced by the richness
of birdlife.

Acknowledgments are difficult to limit—there are so
many people who have helped, directly or indirectly. My
parents took me on a great number of field trips throughout
the State when I was starting to learn about New Jersey
birds. Bill Alston provided a teacher's encouragement in
outdoor biology at Princeton High School and was my first
partner in New Jersey Christmas counts. A strong interest
in avian ecology was generated by Dr. John Trainer at
Muhlenberg College and in summer work with the National
Audubon Society. Graduate studies in ornithology at Cornell
University included two years of research on neotropical
birds. By good fortune I returned to New Jersey and found
a host of outstanding colleagues in the ecology program at
Rutgers University. Within this group Dr. Paul Pearson has
been an especially strong supporter of my studies on New
Jersey's natural bird communities. Thanks are extended also
to many co-operative observers who contributed directly or
through the publications of regional clubs (especially the
Delaware Valley Ornithological Club, the Urner Club, the
Linnaean Society, and the many State clubs and Audubon
societies). I wish to thank also those persons who kindly
gave the manuscript critical readings. The cost of some of
the fieldwork studies in this book was supported by grants
from the Rutgers University Research Council and the
American Philosophical Society.

Introduction

The Birdlife of New Jersey—
An Analysis of the State's Avifauna
by Habitat

Almost all State bird books review the regional avifauna
in a taxonomic order, and, while this is quite useful, the time
has come for a more ecological approach. I have attempted
this approach by considering New Jersey's birdlife in habitat divisions—such as birds of the ocean, birds of the fields,
and so forth. It is a natural organization and gives an inte-
grated view of actual avian communities. Another innovation
is the emphasis (in this section of the book) on the common
or dominant species for each habitat. It is the common birds
that are ecologically important.

The habitats are reviewed by a geographic organization: the Coastal Plain, Piedmont Region, and Highlands
Region as shown on Map 1. For each habitat, I discuss the
birds of a given locale, one that is representative and well
known. The use of specific locations permits more accurate
descriptions of the birdlife than would be possible otherwise.
Further, these bird-watching areas are all preserved for the
future and are thus accessible to the reader. Included are
several State parks and State forests, two National Wildlife
refuges, a city park, and two university properties. Since
1957, I have been on hundreds of field trips to these areas

MAP 1 Ornithological Zones of New Jersey.

at all times of the year—on research projects, class trips, bird-watching tour groups, and bird-banding studies.

Throughout the book the following terms used by field observers appear: *abundant*—a bird species that is usually seen often and in large numbers; *common*—a species that is seen frequently in the appropriate season; *uncommon*—a species that is infrequently seen by the field observer; and *accidental*—a species that does not normally occur in New Jersey. Roughly speaking, an *abundant* bird can be seen daily and a *common* species weekly in season, an *uncommon* species several times a season, a *rare* species only once or twice a season, and an *accidental* species usually less than once a year.

Breeding species are defined here as those actually recorded with nest and eggs. Some authors include observations of juvenile birds as *breeding* records, but this can be questionable in studies of State distributions since juveniles wander widely.

Outline of Habitat Discussions

I. Coastal Plain
  A. Ocean and beach — Island Beach State Park (Chapter 1)
  B. Dunes and thickets — Island Beach State Park
  C. Salt-water marsh — Brigantine National Wildlife Refuge (Chapter 2)
  D. Fresh-water pools — Brigantine National Wildlife Refuge
  E. Coastal upland — Brigantine National Wildlife Refuge
  F. Pine forests — The Pine Barrens (Chapter 3)
  G. Streams and ponds — The Pine Barrens
  H. Cedar swamps — The Pine Barrens

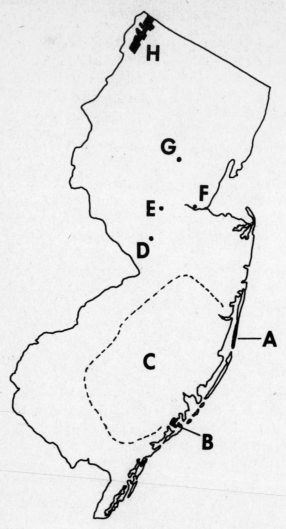

MAP 2 Location of the communities discussed in the text. (A) Island Beach State Park, (B) Brigantine National Wildlife Refuge, (C) The Pine Barrens, (D) Institute Woods and Princeton Wildlife Refuge, (E) Hutcheson Memorial Forest and Fields, (F) Johnson Park, New Brunswick, (G) Great Swamp National Wildlife Refuge, and (H) High Point State Park and Stokes State Forest.

PART I

*Avian Communities
of New Jersey*

CHAPTER ONE

Island Beach State Park

Island Beach State Park consists of the southern ten miles of an undisturbed barrier beach, bounded by the Atlantic Ocean on the east and Barnegat Bay on the west. Natural vegetation covers most of the 2,300 park acres. The plant communities of this sandy area are fairly simple: less than one hundred species comprise the bulk of the vegetation. The plant communities parallel the shore. Sand dunes adjoining the beach are dominated by beach grass (*Ammophila breviligulata*), while succeeding dunes produce hudsonia (*Hudsonia tomentosa*), poison ivy (*Rhus radicans*), bayberry (*Myrica pensylvanica*), cherry (*Prunus serotina*), greenbrier (*Smilax rotundifolia*), and Virginia creeper (*Parthenocissus quinquefolia*). All of the berry-producing shrubs are important sources of food for birds.

Further from the ocean appear trees of low profile: red cedar (*Juniperus virginiana*), holly (*Ilex opaca*), and various species of oak (*Quercus* sp.). On the border of the bay salt grasses dominate (*Phragmites communis* and *Spartina* sp.).

Since 1956 the park has been the center of a very active bird-banding program (Operation Recovery). The co-operation of many bird-banders in the migration seasons, especially in the fall, has contributed greatly to the general knowledge of New Jersey birds. In an eight-year period

(1961–69) a total of 179,191 birds was banded at Island Beach. The park itself is one of the richest areas of birdlife in the State—more than 280 species have been recorded there.

OCEAN AND BEACH

Ocean and beach bird-watching is best conducted in the central recreational zone, 3½ miles south of the park entrance. Parking space is available at either of the two well-marked lots (Units 1 and 2). The beach is directly adjacent to the parking lots.

During spring and fall migrations, hundreds of Common Loons can be counted as they pass by the park, just offshore. The best vantage point for watching the loons is the high beach area near the dunes, where an observer can easily scan the ocean. The greatest number of flights occur in November, when small groups continually fly south along the park shore. In winter months the Red-throated Loon occurs in the surf, catching small fishes. During this period of the year, the dull-colored Red-throated Loons can be best identified by their habit of holding their head upward, with bill skyward. The bird is often quite close to shore and hidden among the breaking waves, so a careful search is usually necessary. When loons are swimming off shore, bird watchers can bring the birds closer by waving a handkerchief or jacket to excite their curiosity. I have seen oil-soaked loons actually walk onto the beach, but they have great difficulty in moving on land. Their legs are set far to the rear of the body for efficient swimming, making walking difficult. Other ocean ducks sharing the surf with the loons include the White-winged, Common, and Surf scoters. In New Jersey the scoters are associated with migration periods and winter; only a few sick or injured birds remain in summer. They can occur in large numbers, particularly in fall, when thousands migrate past the park each hour in characteristically long lines. Because the flocks fly rather far from shore a telescope (twenty-power) is almost essential for accurate counts and specific identification. Their migration routes take them across Canada for nesting in the far west. Along the New Jersey coast in winter, feeding groups or "rafts" approach the shore while diving to catch small fishes or mollusks. These birds can be easily studied from the shore with binoculars, and they often attract other species of waterfowl such as the Oldsquaw. The activities of all the ducks in the flock are often co-ordinated—there are separate periods for feeding, preening, and sleeping. Sleeping scoters bob up and down with the waves, their heads resting on their backs. They seem to sleep lightly and often open their eyes or paddle briefly.

On the beach the most common shorebird is the Sanderling, which forages as close as it can to the edge of the water (Photo 1-1). It retreats at full speed in front of each wave, only to charge forth again as the wave recedes. This ephemeral zone of wet sand provides the tiny crustaceans that form the diet of this beach bird, which is distributed around the world.

Herring Gulls and Ring-billed Gulls are also very common on the beach. As elsewhere along the Atlantic coast, gulls have increased in number by exploiting man's garbage, particularly at coastal dumps. Both gulls are also resourceful in their use of the park's parking lots; these asphalt areas provide a firm substrate for cracking clams. A gull will fly from the beach with a live surf clam that is tightly closed, cross over the dunes and rise above the parking lots, then drop the clam. After falling from a height of fifty or sixty

1-1 The Sanderling. *Photograph by the author*

feet, the clam shatters on the pavement, and the gull has gained its meal. Such behavior shows an intelligent use of the pavement as a feeding "tool." This habit has unpleasant side effects when a fast-falling clam hits a car rather than the pavement itself! Other gulls that appear in summer are the Laughing Gulls, which may be recognized by their black heads and raucous "laugh like" calls. The Laughing Gulls nest toward the bay side of the park, using piles of dead reed grass.

In the summer months the Common Tern (Photo 1-2) and Least Tern may also be seen; both nest at the park (the latter is an endangered species in New Jersey). These fishing birds nest in dense groups on a barren stretch of beach. Unfortunately they are rather sensitive to disturbance, particularly by motorcycles, beach-buggies, and other vehicles that invade the dunes. Even walking through a colony can create havoc as the birds leave their nests and eggs and rapidly become overheated in the direct summer sun. Nesting terns vigorously defend their colony, however, flying about any intruder and threatening him with constant dives and occasional pecks. They also leave a visitor spattered with "white-wash" after their repeated dives. As the young develop through the summer, adults are busy feeding them —in fact most of the terns flying over the beach are carrying small fishes in their bills to their nestlings. Even after the young are able to fly the parent birds continue to feed them for several weeks, since the required skill in catching fish is slowly developed.

In fall migration several other terns appear offshore. The most regular of these is the large Royal Tern, which reaches its normal northern limit in distribution along the New Jersey coast, although September hurricanes push some northward to New England. It suggests a gull in flight, but

1-2 The Common Tern. The bird is sitting on eggs, shading them from the hot summer sun. *Photograph by Allan D. Cruickshank from National Audubon Society*

its bright orange bill and black cap distinguish it clearly. I usually see the Royal Tern in small groups that co-operate in finding fish—when one bird is successful it gives a loud call that attracts the others of the group.

DUNES AND WOODLAND THICKETS

The dunes and thickets are strictly protected and should be used for bird-watching only on guided tours of the park service or on well-marked public trails, indicated by park signs. The Aeolium Nature Trail and Ecology Trail are excellent. Further information can be obtained at the park office.

The most outstanding avian phenomenon of Island Beach State Park is the spectacular fall migration, when thousands of land birds pour through this coastal strip each day. The vegetation is literally alive with birds moving along the park. The height of migration occurs in late September and October. The birds are especially numerous towards the bay where holly, oak, and pine thickets border the open dunes (Photo 1-3). Birds that are migrating to the southeast are concentrated along the shore because of a "boundary effect"—migrants are reluctant to fly out over the ocean, so they pile up and move south along the coast.

Included among these migrants are the birds of prey, two of which are quite rare elsewhere in the State—the Peregrine Falcon and Pigeon Hawk (or Merlin). Pigeon Hawks are actually small falcons that feed on birds smaller than pigeons—I have seen one make a fast dive to try to take a Starling from a flock. Usually they move over the dunes in little circles as they soar on sea winds. Another small falcon, the Sparrow Hawk, is probably the most common predatory bird of the park. The Sparrow Hawks regu-

1-3　A natural area of the Island Beach State Park. The woods and thickets in the background are the site of the "Operation Recovery" bird-banding project. *Photograph by the author*

larly perch along the park's road on telephone wires. In sport, they even chase butterflies among the dunes.

Park visitors will also notice enormous stick nests atop telephone poles along the central roadway. These are nests of the "fishing hawk," the Osprey (Photo 1-4). Unfortunately, these birds are not successful in producing young. They lay abnormally thin-shelled eggs that break during incubation, well before hatching time; the eggshell deficiency is caused by a pesticide-induced hormonal upset (birds ingest the pesticides by eating contaminated bay fishes). The pesticides not only affect the Osprey; other predatory birds such as the Peregrine Falcon and Bald Eagle share its reproductive plight. The State of New Jersey has had some success in enabling its nesting Ospreys to breed by providing them with healthy eggs from Chesapeake Bay birds. This new management technique has been successful elsewhere in heavily polluted environments.

Among the smaller fall migrants are Yellow-shafted Flickers (120), which bound over the low vegetation, while Yellow-bellied Sapsuckers (50) perch vertically on small trees. (The numbers in parentheses indicate the maximum that might be mist-netted—Photo 1-5—and banded with "Operation Recovery" at the park in one day.) When banding there, I have noted that the sapsuckers frequently smell of balsam sap—apparently they had just arrived from the north, where they had fed on balsam firs. The little Downy Woodpecker is well represented while foraging on small trees or even reed grass. Woodpeckers in general are not a favorite with bird-banders since the woodpecker tongue, very long and barbed at the tip, useful in catching insects, is often caught in the mist-nets.

Blue Jays are common, but the migrating flocks are usually taller than the vegetation, and they are not caught

I-4 An Osprey on its nest. *Photograph by George W. Leck*

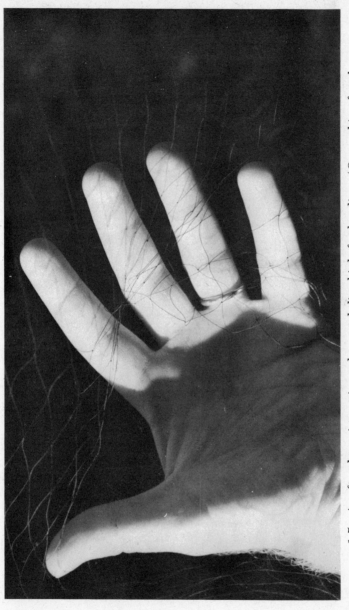

1-5 A soft nylon mist-net is used to catch live birds for banding. (Ownership of such nets requires both State and Federal permits.) *Photograph by the author*

by banders. Many people living in New Jersey are surprised
that the jays are migratory; the birds we see in summer are
replaced by different individuals in winter. It is even more
surprising to learn that the Blue Jay is not strictly "blue"
—the feathers produce only a reflected color because there
is no blue pigment. In general, most "blue" colorations in
the bird world are of this reflective type.

Both the White-breasted Nuthatch (70) and Red-
breasted Nuthatch (100) are numerous. Whereas these are
vocal species inland, they seem silent on their migration
along the barrier beach park. The Red-breasted Nuthatch
is the more social of the two and often migrates in small
groups. Also silent is the Brown Creeper, which reaches
maximum abundance in early October, when I have banded
more than a hundred in two hours. This abundance is particularly impressive when compared with inland counts,
which seldom yield more than a dozen a day. The creepers
and nuthatches overlap in their feeding zones—each species
searches for insects on the bark of small trees—but the
creeper always spirals upward from the base of the trunk,
while the nuthatch moves head-first down the tree. The
nuthatch also includes seeds in its diet. In fact, the name
nuthatch is a corruption of the old English name for the
bird, "Nuthack," which describes their habit of hacking the
seeds they are about to eat.

Catbirds (200), Brown Thrashers (50), Swainson's
Thrushes (150), Gray-cheeked Thrushes (100) are all
common migrants. The thrushes can be easily heard at night
giving soft "chip" notes on their flight south; the notes permit
the birds to remain together as a flock on their journey
through the dark. Formerly it was claimed that the "chip"
notes permitted specific identifications, but this now seems
an exaggeration for any but the most proficient field work-

ers. The nocturnal habits of migrants such as the thrushes have led to interesting research on the "cues" used by these birds. It is now established by field and planetarium research that some species actually use star patterns for their navigation. During the height of migration a thrush may fly 200 to 300 miles a night to reach its northern breeding grounds, using large amounts of body fat as fuel. The heavy fat deposits of migrants are obvious on mist-netted birds as the yellowish adipose tissue is just under the thin skin.

In early October the tiny Golden-crowned (200) and Ruby-crowned kinglets (100) are common, but rapidly decline in number by the end of the month. Only the Golden-crowned remains in small numbers through the winter. On one field trip we saw kinglets flying in from over the ocean and falling from exhaustion on the first dunes, or even landing on our shoulders. They suffered from dehydration and eagerly accepted canteen water—a great amount of body water is used in flight. Many of these tiny migrants die when blown seaward on their fall flights. But their mortality losses are offset by survivors during the next breeding season—the kinglets raise seven to nine young a brood.

When one is banding it becomes obvious that the name Red-eyed Vireo (100) is appropriate only for the adult bird —juveniles have brown eyes that sometimes lead to misidentifications as the more western Bell's Vireo. Warblers are dominated by the Parula (60), the Blackpoll (70), the Palm (70), the Redstart (80), the Yellowthroat (50), and the Myrtle (300). I have seen the Myrtle Warbler on its breeding grounds from Nova Scotia to Alaska, but nowhere is it as abundant as in Island Beach State Park in the fall. In fall and winter the Myrtle Warbler changes its diet from insects to bayberries and is thus New Jersey's only winter warbler. The other warblers mentioned above are also of special note: the Parula is New Jersey's smallest warbler, less than four inches in length; the Blackpoll is a very long-distance migrant, flying well into South America in winter; the tail-wagging Palm is the most terrestrial warbler, almost entirely restricted to ground feeding; the bright Redstart is the most sexually dimorphic (difference between male and female plumages) warbler; and the Yellowthroat is one of the State's earliest migrants, as most pass through Island Beach by the first week of September.

Other common migrants are in the finch family. Most abundant of these are the Slate-colored Junco (700) and the White-throated Sparrow (600). Both of these breed in evergreen forests north of New Jersey, but they appear in the park from October to May. In spring, as the breeding season approaches, both species begin singing before they leave the coast. The slow crisp whistles of the White-throated Sparrow may be heard clearly in the bay-side shrubbery, whereas the junco gives a simple trill. Birds that are less than one year old practice with somewhat imperfect songs that improve with age. Other common sparrows that are netted for banding include the Rufous-sided Towhee (120), the Swamp Sparrow (50), and the Song Sparrow (100). The towhee is the most colorful of these, with distinctive patterns of black, brown, rusty, and white. Towhee colors are geographically variable: western birds have spotted backs (the "spotted towhee") and southern birds white rather than red eyes (the "white-eyed towhee"). Young towhees, unlike the adults, have streaked brown and buff plumage. In fall the juveniles molt into adult colors. Song Sparrows show even greater variation over the continent, with pale-colored birds in arid areas, dark birds in humid regions, and larger birds at higher latitudes. Such variations are specific adaptations to environment. Most of the members of the finch family at the park can be seen best in late spring when they establish nesting territories and sing from conspicuous perches.

As one would expect, the great amount of bird-banding and bird-watching activity at the park has turned up a great many rarities along with the common species mentioned above. Of the sparrows, for example, the western Clay-colored and Lark sparrows are both recorded annually, and the first Lincoln's Sparrow I saw in New Jersey was at my Island Beach mist-net. The netting program reveals far more rarities than would be found by direct observation, because the nets sample large areas continuously.

CHAPTER TWO

Brigantine National Wildlife Refuge

On the New Jersey coastal marsh, just eleven miles north of Atlantic City, is one of the most heavily visited wildlife refuges in the United States (Photo 2-1). The nearly 20,000 acres of the Brigantine National Wildlife Refuge include salt marsh (about 75 per cent of the total), upland brush and forest, and two man-made fresh-water pools (700 and 900 acres). The easternmost portion of the refuge borders the Atlantic Ocean and is accessible only by boat, but roads and trails provide excellent bird-watching opportunities in all major habitats of the western section. The isolated eastern portion has been proposed as a National Wilderness Area so that it can remain undisturbed. The refuge provides a number of facilities including a reporting station for bird watchers with informative checklists and pamphlets.

The salt-marsh vegetation includes vast expanses of the low marsh hay (*Spartina patens*), with smooth cord grass (*Spartina alterniflora*) along drainage ditches. In the marsh, hay flats, black grass (*Juncus gerardi*), salt grass (*Distichlis spicata*), and saltworts (*Salicornia*) are common. On raised ground the seaside goldenrod (*Solidago sempervirens*) appears and marsh elder (*Iva frutescens*) is abundant. A

2-1 View from an observation tower at Brigantine National Wildlife Refuge. *Photograph by the author*

variety of the salt-marsh birds nest only on areas of high ground.

Where fresh water exerts an influence, reed grass (*Phragmites communis*) and bulrushes (*Scirpus*) invade. Important food plants for ducks have been introduced in the fresh-water ponds. The sandy upland pine forest contains much the same plant community as the Pine Barrens, described in the next chapter.

FRESH-WATER POOLS AND SALT-WATER AREAS

From Route 9 at Oceanville, the entrance road to the Brigantine Refuge leads directly to headquarters, which has maps of the refuge on display. The single road from headquarters continues on an eight-mile loop, with fresh-water pools continually on the left, and salt-water areas on the right.

The aquatic birdlife of the Brigantine Refuge is not surpassed anywhere in New Jersey, and, in fact, few if any areas of the East Coast can be as exciting. An example of this diversity is in the heron family, with ten species nesting at the refuge. The herons each have a specialized feeding niche: the Great Blue Heron wades in deep water for large fishes; the Common Egret (Photo 2-2) waits for moderate-sized fish; the Cattle Egret forages on high ground for grasshoppers and other large insects; the Little Blue Heron snatches small fish from shallow water or canals; the Green Heron waits motionlessly for fish near a log or bank; the Snowy Egret actively chases schools of small fishes; the American Bittern snatches frogs from the reeds; the Least Bittern feeds on insects on the reeds; the Louisiana Heron remains in pools; the Black-crowned and Yellow-crowned Night herons divide the fishes in the evening hours. Such

2-2 The Common Egret (also known as the Great Egret), symbol of the National Audubon Society. *Photograph by the author*

specialization by closely related birds is a common ecological phenomenon—it allows for less competition for food.

Several details of these feeding strategies deserve further comment. The active pursuit of fish by the Snowy Egret is always filled with antics. The bird rushes about in circles, waving its golden feet in the water to keep the fish moving. It periodically opens its wings over the water and then suddenly closes them, perhaps using sunlight to startle the prey. And it lunges at the swimming fish with its whole body. In contrast, the Common Egret maintains a distinguished upright attitude while waiting for prey to pass by. It does become disheveled, however, if the prey is an eel, when it may find its bill wrapped in the coils of a rather slippery item. I have watched a Common Egret swallowing a freshly caught eel for more than half an hour, with heron antics that rivalled those of the Snowy Egret. The Common Egret was once at the verge of extinction because of the plume-hunting millinery trade, but efforts of the National Audubon Society saved the species.

The most terrestrial heron, the Cattle Egret, is a recent invader of North America, apparently spreading naturally from Africa into the New World via South America—the bird has excellent powers of sustained flight. Its numbers have increased tremendously since 1958, its first year of nesting in New Jersey. It is still increasing its range in the United States and simultaneously in Africa and Australia—there has been some rapid biological change that has made this possible, but it remains a mystery.

Another wader that is increasing in number is the spectacular Glossy Ibis, for which Brigantine is famous. Its dark plumage with metallic sheen and long curved beak make it easily recognizable. In summer several hundred may be observed at the refuge, and these have provided the basic stock for further expansion, even into Long Island. The ibis family is a very old one—millions of years old—and the birds still have a prehistoric appearance, with a flight form reminiscent of flying reptiles. The worldwide ibis family also has provided the oldest known bird specimens, including mummified Sacred Ibis found in the ancient pyramids. The herons, egrets, and ibis all nest together in an apartmentlike colony in a small forest. As in feeding, there is distinct segregation of the different species—for example, the Great Blue Herons nest near the tree tops, while the Snowy Egrets build at eye level, and the ibis construct a platform of sticks on the ground or on the lowest limbs.

Another recent addition to the area is the Mute Swan, a species introduced from Europe at the beginning of this century. It is a nesting resident at the refuge and is the heaviest flying bird in the world, with adult males weighing up to forty pounds. Nesting swans are quite aggressive and should not be disturbed—a rapid blow from one of their wings can break a child's leg. Most Mute Swans in New Jersey are domesticated in parks, but the Brigantine birds are truly feral. In England there were elaborate systems of marking the bills of captive Mute Swans to show ownership—systems that reflect local heraldry and the ordinances of the country (consolidated by the Act of the Swans in 1482). While American Mute Swans lack protective legislation, they are seldom taken by hunters, since most of the birds allow close approach and are not a challenge to hunt.

Other waterfowl form a major group of the avifauna at Brigantine, although few species nest there. The breeding birds include the common species—Mallard, Black Duck, Gadwall, Pintail, Blue-winged Teal, Shoveler, Wood Duck, and Ruddy Duck. These ducks include some of the top game species of the State. The downy young are evident in July and August, with their fuzzy plumage of browns, creams, white, and black, according to the species. The duckling's down is changed to a juvenile plumage during the summer. The young are well developed when hatched and increasingly wander from the hen as they mature. When danger threatens, however, all are quick to run or swim at top speed back to the parent. Adult ducks recognize their own young by their coloration and distinctive peep calls. The exaggerated independence of the young ducklings while feeding provides a humorous contrast to their instant dependence on the mother when approached. The hen of any duck species shows extreme dedication to her brood; if one of the young becomes caught in vegetation or an animal trap she will remain with it and circle it until the duckling is dead. Fortunately, such dramas are rare in the undisturbed environment of the refuge, but animal traps still take their toll of waterfowl elsewhere.

Since "shooting" ducks with a camera has become as popular as hunting them with a gun, the refuge has built blinds for photographers at the edge of the waterfowl pools. The nesting waterfowl approach the blinds, even with young, if the photographer remains quiet inside. Sometimes it is necessary to fool the birds when using a blind by having two people enter and then one leave: birds are unable to count.

Many more Anseriformes (from the Latin for gooselike) appear at the refuge during the migration periods and winter. Geese are represented by the Canada Goose, symbol of the National Wildlife Refuges (Photo 2-3), the smaller Brant, the Snow Goose, and the Blue Goose. The large Canada Geese are present in moderate numbers each year, and a small number remain to breed at the refuge in summer (Photo 2-4). The geese select mates when two years old

2-3 A welcome sign to many bird watchers, the "flying goose" of the Federal refuges. *Photograph by the author*

2-4 A Canada Goose nesting box at Brigantine National Wildlife Refuge. *Photograph by the author*

and remain paired for life. However, most Canada Geese and all of the other three species depart for breeding grounds in the far north, on Canadian tundra. For some, the migration journey may span 4,000 miles. The Brant fluctuate in numbers from year to year, but they are often the most abundant geese at the refuge; in fact, Brigantine Bay holds more Brants than any area of comparable size. The species suffered a drastic decline in number earlier in the century when its favorite food plant, eel grass, was almost eliminated by a blight. Brants turned to other aquatic vegetation for food and fortunately survived. Today the noisy flocks of thousands consume a wide variety of marine algae in the shallow waters of the refuge. The Snow Geese now rival the Brant in abundance at Brigantine, although they are relatively new to the refuge. In the 1960s Snow Geese appeared in increasing numbers with each successive winter, apparently shifting their normal wintering area from the Delaware Bay to the Atlantic coast. Now Snow Geese number in the thousands, much to the delight of bird watchers— few other areas on the Atlantic coast attract the bird. The species may be too successful at the refuge; the wildlife management believes they may be overgrazing the local salt marsh, leading to serious tidal erosion. Amid the thousands of Snow Geese one can usually find a few Blue Geese— patience, with some caution, is required, as a *young* Snow Goose can resemble the rarer Blue Goose. Recent field research has shown these two geese to be a single species, in spite of the color variations. Thus, Blue Geese mate with Snow Geese in the wild and produce mixed progeny according to the genetic laws of simple inheritance. In fact, I have seen clear "hybrids" of the Blue and Snow geese wintering at Brigantine. The flocks of Snow Geese can best be enjoyed during their morning and late afternoon flights into and out of the refuge pools. Beautiful white flocks pass close overhead with constant honking.

In addition to the breeding ducks mentioned earlier, the Green-winged Teal and American Widgeon are common in the fresh-water pools. Although both species nest further north, they court and form pairs at the refuge before spring migration. At wooded Lily Pond, migrant Ring-necked Ducks appear temporarily in fall and spring flocks. Since the 1930s, this species has increased its frequency of appearance in New Jersey, but it is still uncommon. In salt-water areas, especially in the bay, many other waterfowl are prevalent. The Common Goldeneye, the Bufflehead, and Greater Scaup dominate, with lesser numbers of scoters and mergansers. Paradoxically, the least common of the three scoters is called the Common Scoter, and the least common of the three mergansers is known as the Common Merganser. These provide simple examples of the anomalies that ornithologists hope to correct by using names based on plumage or some other permanent characteristic. For example, it has been proposed that the Common Scoter be renamed the Black Scoter, as it is already known in England.

Birds of prey seen over the refuge ponds include the Osprey and Marsh Hawk, the latter sailing low over the marsh vegetation in search of a meadow mouse or frog. In spring the Marsh Hawks sometimes engage in spectacular courtship flights at the refuge. A male rises above the salt-marsh to a height of eighty feet or more, slowly stalls, and then plunges into a sharp dive, only to pull out within several yards of the ground. The bird continues with an immediate climb, and the sequence is repeated, often with five or six dives in a row. The most dramatic displays seem to occur on windy days, in the afternoon. Several rarer birds of prey make regular appearances—the Golden and Bald eagles have been seen at the Brigantine Refuge on the same day. In the late 1950s and 1960s I saw Bald Eagles on more than half of my trips to the refuge—a record that could not be matched in other parts of the State except at the Kitta-tinny Mountains. More recently, one of the few Gyrfalcons ever recorded in New Jersey appeared at the refuge and attracted more than 150 observers from six states. I saw this hawk swiftly attack and devour a male Green-winged Teal with incredible skill. In fact, the Gyrfalcon, the largest falcon in the world, is eagerly sought by falconers, who will pay up to $2,000 for a trained bird (in medieval times only kings were allowed to own Gyrfalcons).

Coots (Photo 2-5) are obvious in the fresh-water pools and attract the attention of visitors. Amid the salt-marsh flats the seldom-seen Clapper Rails are abundant: their train-like call, "choo-choo-choo," is heard throughout the breed-ing season in every part of the refuge. At the turn of the century Clapper Rails, in spite of their poor flavor, were being slaughtered for food markets by hunters at the rate of more than ten thousand a year in the region of Brigantine. Even today, the rails still show a strong aversion to people —they frantically dash into the salt-marsh grass when sighted.

Shorebirds are a great attraction at the refuge: more than thirty-seven species have been seen there in recent years, exceeding recent records for the whole of any other eastern state. This chapter's review of the common shore-birds only hints at the excitement possible in searching for this group. The largest shorebird of all is the American Oystercatcher with its spectacular red bill—yes, it does use its bill to open bivalves such as oysters and other mollusks. Occasionally an oyster clamps on the bill and the bird starves to death. The species reaches the northernmost limit

2-5 Coots have heavy bodies and must build momentum by running across the water before they can take off in flight. *Photograph by George W. Leck*

of its breeding grounds near the refuge, although some believe that its range will soon include southern Long Island.
The favorite location of New Jersey's Oystercatchers is just
north of Brigantine at Tuckerton (Photo 2-6), adjacent to
the Rutgers University field station for marine work. As
with most shorebirds, the Oystercatcher's daily activity is
closely synchronized with local tidal rhythms—they are most
active on the exposed mud flats at low tide.

Common plovers are the Semipalmated and its larger
relative the Killdeer, as well as the migrant Black-bellied
Plover (Photo 2-7). The latter, as with so many shorebird
species, is well named for its attractive spring plumage,
which bears little resemblance to its dull fall coloration.
(The breeding-season coloration of birds is generally known
as the nuptial plumage; the winter plumage succeeds the
fall molt.) The Ruddy Turnstone is another common migrant
at the refuge, on its way to or from the far north. It too is
far more attractive in its bright nuptial plumage than in
its brown winter garb. At the edge of the bay migrant turn-
stones establish individual feeding territories that are defended vigorously by aggressive chases.

Salt-marsh flats also attract breeding Willets, another
large shorebird. Because they are so plain Willets sometimes
pose identification problems until they give their loud call,
"will-will-willet," or raise their white banded wings, a field
mark reflected in the bird's scientific name *Catoptrophorus*,
mirror-wing. In the fall some individuals are noticeably
larger and paler—these are Willets from the western states.
Other common shorebirds include the Yellowlegs, Least
Sandpiper, Dunlin (the "winter sandpiper"), Short-billed
Dowitcher, Semipalmated Sandpiper, and the breeding
Spotted Sandpiper. The Dunlin, formerly called the Red-
backed Sandpiper, greatly outnumbers all other sandpipers

2-6 The famous Tuckerton salt marshes—a vast expanse of spartina grass, with tidal flats. (A fish factory is on the horizon.) *Photograph by the author*

2-7 The Black-bellied Plover in winter plumage. *Photograph by H. M. Halliday from National Audubon Society*

after November. It is highly gregarious and flocks in thousands. Its tameness led to massive slaughters in the open hunting of the 1890s. There are many other interesting species, and one of these deserves particular mention, the American Avocet. Generally rare on the East Coast, this species nested in New Jersey before the turn of the century. It is now hoped that the Brigantine visitors may settle down to breed. I once counted eighteen in the West Pool, and recent reports include one flock of sixty.

Gulls and terns are plentiful also. The following breeding birds are common in the refuge—the Laughing Gull, Common Tern, and Least Tern. The gull prefers to nest in matted vegetation debris on the salt marsh, while the terns are satisfied with simple depressions near an abandoned dune. During summer Forster's Terns patrol the canals for small fish. When a fish is noted the tern begins hovering and then plunges directly downward with folded wings. They nest in small numbers at the periphery of the refuge, constructing floating mats of marsh reeds that move with the tides. During fall migrations the Black Tern sometimes appears in small groups at the fresh-water pools. They fly with deep wing-beats and often utter sharp "keek" calls. This tern contrasts markedly with other terns in its black summer plumage and noncoastal breeding range; it nests in the prairie states and Canadian provinces. The Black Tern also differs in its manner of feeding—it plucks food from the surface of pools instead of diving.

Finally there is the Black Skimmer (Photo 2-8). The mixed diurnal and nocturnal habits of the bird require great accommodation by its eyes, and it is the only bird in the world with a catlike slit iris rather than a round pupil. Its unusual habit of skimming the water with its lower beak to catch small fishes or invertebrates also requires special

2-8 The Black Skimmer. *Photograph by the author*

adaptations, particularly of the head bones and neck muscles. There is an ingenious "trip mechanism" at the base of the skull, for example, that prevents damage if the bill hits a submerged object such as a log. This safety feature is obvious when a foraging skimmer rapidly snaps its head backwards and continues unharmed, even if it hits a sandbar. The skimmer is a southern bird that has recently expanded its range, nesting as far north as Long Island. There are few colonies in New Jersey; the largest is on the Holgate peninsula of the Brigantine Refuge. I have counted more than fifty there from the *edge* of the colony (to avoid serious disturbance of their nesting one should never enter the actual breeding area).

Upland Areas

The upland areas of Brigantine Refuge have trail signs along the single-tour road, with appropriate parking areas. Excellent upland bird-watching may be enjoyed along the foot trails about the Refuge Headquarters, including the clearly marked Nature Trail.

Birds of the upland areas of the Brigantine National Wildlife Refuge are similar to those of the forests of the Pine Barrens. Man-made clearings and fields are important at the refuge, however. Stocked Bobwhites and Ring-necked Pheasants are common along wood edges and benefit from some of the cultivated grasses. Both venture into open fields, but only the pheasants allow bird watchers to approach closely. Bobwhites usually avoid man or other predators by running away at high speed, and they can also take off in a burst of flight at greater than forty miles an hour.

Other common nesting residents include the Mourning Dove, Yellow-shafted Flicker, and Downy Woodpecker.

Among the passerines there are at least forty more breeding birds that can be considered common. Flycatchers include the Great-crested Flycatcher and Eastern Phoebe. The Phoebe is apparently limited in its distribution by its fondness for streams—it rarely nests far from running water. Tree Swallows use nest boxes set up at the fresh-water drainage of Lily Lake, and Purple Martins have a colony in a nest house at the refuge headquarters. The long martin association with man precedes the arrival of Europeans, as Indians formerly attracted the birds with nesting gourds. Both the Blue Jay and Fish Crow are numerous. The Blue Jay is particularly abundant in migration, and the sociable Fish Crow forms sizeable flocks in winter. The Long-billed Marsh Wren nests in secrecy in the reed grass—only its constant calling reveals its presence. Its polygamous males court and pair with several females on their small territories. All species of the mimic family, Mimidae, are easily noted in the upland woods, especially at thickets with berry-bearing hollies. Most numerous are the Catbird, Mockingbird, and Brown Thrasher, in that order, but the Mockingbird is increasing in number. Also among the thickets is the White-eyed Vireo with its ventriloquistic call—a frustration to all bird watchers. The Red-eyed Vireo seems somewhat less common except where oaks predominate and has apparently declined in number in recent years. Its compact nest is a masterpiece of construction, with a lining of hair or soft rootlets, an outside camouflaged with leaves, and binding filaments of spider silk.

Warblers in the upland habitat are dominated by the pine-loving Prairie and Pine warblers; there are a few Black-and-White Warblers that nest on the ground amid the oak leaf litter. In low moist areas or along streams the Yellow Warbler and Yellow-throat appear as summer residents.

Otherwise the refuge, like all of the coastal plain, has little diversity of warblers even in migration periods, because the pines grow out of nearly barren soil.

In 1852 the House Sparrow, also known as the English Sparrow, was introduced from Europe into North America at New York City. It quickly spread through the east and became one of the few abundant urban birds. In suburban areas it concentrates at feeding stations, and this is true at the refuge as well. There, however, it is sometimes snatched by a hungry Sharp-shinned Hawk, a fast-moving predator unfamiliar to the city bird. The unwary sparrow is also known to be the prey of snakes and even large bull frogs.

Among the blackbirds, the Redwinged stands out as being ecologically important throughout the fresh-water marshes as a consumer of insects and seeds. Its numbers grow dramatically when large flocks arrive from the north in late fall. Unfortunately, the Red-winged Blackbird invasion sometimes causes millions of dollars of crop damage to truck gardeners in southern New Jersey.

Finches nest in a variety of habitats about the refuge: old fields (Field Sparrow and American Goldfinch), pine woods (Rufous-sided Towee), salt marsh (Seaside and Sharp-tailed Sparrows), lawns (Chipping Sparrow), and wet thickets (Song and Swamp Sparrows). Again ecological specialization, reducing competition, in this case by habitat, is evident between closely related birds with similar diets. In New Jersey the Seaside and Sharp-tailed sparrows are restricted to the saline habitat typified by the refuge. Although they are common, they remain secretive in the cord grass and their song, a thin trill, attracts little attention. Bird watchers can obtain glimpses if the birds briefly fly when flushed—the Seaside Sparrow appears uniformly dark while the Sharp-tailed Sparrow has a distinctive buffy appearance.

This review dealt with the commoner birds; I have tallied 191 species at Brigantine, and in all more than two hundred and fifty species of birds have been recorded there. It is impossible to predict just what may be found at the refuge. One morning I visited the fresh-water pools at daybreak to see a flock of Fulvous Tree Ducks, a tropical species new for New Jersey. I found six of the ducks swimming out of the reeds, and shortly thereafter was amazed to see four busloads of bird watchers arrive at the scene—the news of the exotic birds had reached a nearby convention of the National Audubon Society. Now Fulvous Tree Ducks are recorded almost annually at the refuge.

CHAPTER THREE

The Pine Barrens

More than one million acres of southern New Jersey are covered with the pine and oak woodlands of the Pine Barrens. This undeveloped area is characterized by its sandy soils and monotonous vegetation—hence the name "Barrens." The upland forests are dominated by the abundant pitch pine (*Pinus rigida*—Photo 3-1) and a number of oaks: blackjack oak (*Quercus marilandica*), bear oak (*Q. ilicifolia*), and post oak (*Q. stellata*). The shrubbery consists of ericaceous plants that are tolerant of the acidic sands, such as laurels (*Kalmia*), huckleberries (*Gaylussacia*), and blueberries (*Vaccinium*). Lowland vegetation is tolerant of moisture—the swamp trees include the majestic Atlantic white-cedar (*Chamaecyparis thyoides*—Photo 3-2), red maple (*Acer rubrum*), and black gum (*Nyssa sylvatica*). Smaller swamp plants featured are rare ferns, sundews, and pitcher plants. Large open ponds, usually surrounded by leatherleaf (*Chamaedaphne*), are common throughout the region.

In contrast with most plant and animal groups of the Barrens, there is a rich diversity of amphibians and reptiles —fifty-three species. These include the unique Pine Barrens tree frog, the carpenter frog, the fence lizard, the northern pine snake, and the beautiful scarlet snake. The reptiles

3-1 The simple forest of the Pine Barrens is dominated by pitch pine. *Photograph by the author*

3-2   The forest of the cedar swamps in the Pine Barrens. *Photograph by the author*

and amphibians both benefit from the moderate climate of southern New Jersey and the sandy soils that allow easy burrowing.

UPLAND PINE FORESTS

Well-marked trails are established in almost all of the State Parks and Forests of the Pine Barrens. Upland pine paths particularly good for bird watchers include the Batsto Park Nature Trail, the Manasquan Trail of Allaire Park, and the sandy roads of Penn State Forest.

Turkey Vultures soar overhead in their search for carrion. The species is quite common in the Pine Barrens and is airborne on any clear day (Photo 3-3). Because it is a gliding species, dependent on rising air currents, it rises skyward by late morning. The vulture is less common in northern New Jersey and is scarce in New England, where it is strictly a summer resident. The southern Black Vulture ventures as far north as Delaware, but only rarely crosses into New Jersey. In contrast with its relative, the Black Vulture is essentially nonmigratory. Both species are found throughout Central and South America. John James Audubon was the first to experiment with the vultures' ability to find food—at one site he placed a painting of a dead deer, at another site only the odor of carrion from a hidden carcass. The odor proved to be the stronger attraction, and this has been recently verified by the research of other ornithologists. Red-tailed Hawks also share the sky, but they search for live prey—rodents and rabbits. This hawk seems most abundant in winter when its prey is most exposed. In early spring the birds pair off in aerial courtship displays. A soaring male approaches a prospective mate and swoops by her with majestic grace, sometimes offering

3-3   The Turkey Vulture. *Photograph by the author*

her a recently caught mouse from his talons. During the courtship a piercing scream, the mating call, can be heard at great distances. The pair builds a bulky nest of sticks that is often used for many years in succession. Both parents incubate the two or three white eggs spotted with brown. Along the road a smaller predator, the Sparrow Hawk, is common. Unlike the large stick-nest of the Red-tailed Hawk, the Sparrow Hawk's nest is a cramped chamber in a tree trunk. The female does most of the incubating of the eggs, and she defends them from any intruder by rolling on her back and raising her sharp talons. "Sparrow Hawk" is actually a misnomer—its diet includes grasshoppers and mice rather than sparrows, and it is a falcon rather than a hawk. This is the only bird of prey in New Jersey that still commonly serves as a falconer's pet. Falcons as a group are distinguished by their pointed wings; the fifty species of the family (falconidae), are distributed throughout the world.

Game birds include the Ruffed Grouse or Partridge, which utilizes a wide variety of plant foods (partridge berries, grapes, and greenbrier berries), as well as many buds. I regularly see grouse along the southern roads, and in general they appear to be doing well in the Barrens, in contrast to their relatives—the Heath Hen was extinct in New Jersey by 1870, the Turkey was extirpated by hunting, and the introduced Bobwhite has often failed to survive. The only consistently common gamebird in the Pine Barrens is the Mourning Dove, although it is not presently on New Jersey's State hunting list. In modern times the Mourning Dove has been aided by man's widespread clearing of the woods and concomitant increase in seed-bearing weeds.

Night birds in the Pine Barrens include the little Screech Owl and the loud-voiced Whip-poor-will. Both can be heard easily during their breeding seasons. I have talked with residents of the Pine Barrens who spent many sleepless nights in June because of the incessant calls of Whip-poor-wills. It is not until its ground nest is completed and two eggs are laid that the Whip-poor-will ceases his calling.

The early summer brings many flowers and Ruby-throated Hummingbirds (Photo 3-4), feeding like bees on the nectar in the flowers. Like the insects, the hummingbird is a pollinating agent for the flowers, transferring pollen that produces cross-fertilization. Only the male has the bright red throat, or gorget, for which the species was named. The red coloration is a structural reflection, almost metallic in appearance, that varies with the angle of the observer. One can best observe the ruby red when males court with pendulumlike swinging flights in the open sunlight; the throat literally flashes in the sunlight. Also, a low hum is heard from the rapid wings (sixty beats a second).

Woodpeckers are represented by three common species —the Yellow-shafted Flicker, which eats ants from the ground, and two closely related tree foragers, the Hairy and Downy woodpeckers. All three excavate cavities in trees, where they lay their white eggs (there is no need for protective coloration of eggs in the dark). They prefer dead trees, since live trees ooze too much sap and make life sticky. Both parent flickers build the large nesting cavity, which is well used by the prolific female. She typically lays six to eight eggs, and there is a report of one bird incubating nineteen eggs. Both male and female Downy Woodpeckers excavate their nest cavity, but among Hairy Woodpeckers the female alone constructs the nursery chamber.

Flycatchers all have selected habitats in the woodlands. The Eastern Kingbird perches and waits for flying

3-4 A male Ruby-throated Hummingbird visits a feeder for sugar water. *Photograph by Donald S. Heintzelman*

insects near a forest opening or at a roadside (Photo 3-5). The kingbird courtship begins with a brief flight close to the ground and graceful dips—it ends with a clutch of four creamy eggs. The Great-crested Flycatcher is heard giving its "wheeep" call from old oak and pine stands. The early American naturalist Mark Catesby described the call as a "brawling noise." The Eastern Phoebe, prevalent in the Barrens, is attracted to old houses or other buildings where it can safely place its delicate cup nest. Its young may be found there in June; late summer fledglings can be recognized by two brownish wing stripes.

Three members of the crow family appear in the Pine Barrens. The Blue Jay benefits from the annual crop of acorns, and the Common Crow from the meat of animals killed along the highways. Both eat almost anything, however, and are described as omnivores. They are also among the most intelligent of birds, with both an extensive vocabulary and elaborate social organization. The third species is the small Fish Crow, which is restricted to the coastal regions of the Pine Barrens, where it frequents tidal rivers. In southern states this crow invades nesting colonies of herons and egrets for eggs but this habit is less apparent in New Jersey.

Other southerners that inhabit the Barrens are the Carolina Chickadee, the Carolina Wren, and the Mockingbird. The thin-voiced Chickadee is a hole-nesting resident; it uses abandoned woodpecker cavities. Audubon first identified this species in Charleston, South Carolina, and thus designated its specific name as *carolinensis*. The musical Carolina Wren nests in brush piles or thickets, where its loud voice can be heard long before the bird is sighted. Like so many great bird songs, the enthusiastic concerts of the Carolina Wren cannot be described adequately—they

3-5 The Eastern Kingbird. *Photograph by G. Ronald Austing from National Audubon Society*

provide strong inducements for bird watchers to buy records of bird songs. Because this wren is nonmigratory it often dies in severe winters. Sometimes females even die from exposure on early spring nests. The Mockingbird is of course a highly accomplished singer as well. With the turn of the century the Mockingbird first invaded New Jersey through the Pine Barrens and is now widely distributed and often abundant. The species has simultaneously expanded southward into the West Indies, where its success also seems assured—Mockingbirds are highly resourceful and sufficiently aggressive to dominate other birds. Even at northern feeding stations it is obvious that the Mockingbird can rebuff larger species.

In forested areas with shrubbery the Brown Thrasher searches for insects or chases a young fence lizard. While a rapid runner, the Brown Thrasher is one of the slowest flyers, rarely exceeding twenty miles an hour. Even the common Robin can easily fly twice as fast. Both species produce two broods a year, laying four to five eggs for each.

Insect-eaters in the pine lands include the vireos and warblers. In this region the common Red-eyed Vireo is associated with stands of young oaks, but it is certainly less numerous than in the forests of northern New Jersey. Because the oak woodlands are relatively open, the vireos become inactive in the mid-day heat of the Barrens. Warblers include the abundant Pine Warbler, the Prairie Warbler, the Black-and-White Warbler, and the ground nesting Ovenbird. In early May the pleasant trill of the Pine Warbler can be heard through the day in almost any part of the Pine Barrens. Its compact nest of bark, pine needles, and spider webs is often located near the top of a pine tree. I find it best to hike into the quieter areas to find the Prairie and Pine warblers, but recommend caution

—it is easy to become lost in the monotonous pitch-pine habitat.

The family to which finches and sparrows belong includes the most abundant kind of bird in the Pine Barrens, the Rufous-sided Towhee. This species is said to outnumber all others as a nesting resident, and indeed it does seem ubiquitous. Males court by spreading and closing their wings and tails to show the white markings. The females build the nests. Near clearings or old fields the American Goldfinch flocks to breed. The male of this species is more helpful, even bringing food to his incubating mate. Other common finches are winter visitors such as the Evening Grosbeak and Pine Siskin. All of these winter birds flock; the siskins are often with groups of goldfinches. After a few winter hikes in the Pine Barrens, the bird watcher can become proficient in identifying finches, since many give distinctive calls. The northern-nesting finches remain in the Pine Barrens until late spring. Even in mid-May Red Crossbills and Pine Siskins wander about the region. But by the end of the month these all disappear, and only the few resident finches remain.

STREAMS

Some of the best vegetation and birdlife of the Pine Barrens is found along the Batsto River in Wharton State Forest and MacDonald's Branch in Lebanon Forest. Road maps or park maps show several locations adjacent to well-marked roads. Canoeing along the Wading River in Burlington County is highly rewarding, especially in late spring.

Along the slow and shallow streams of the Pine Barrens the vegetation is thick, and a number of additional bird species appear. Catbirds, Yellow Warblers, Yellowthroats, and Field Sparrows nest along stream banks and make themselves evident to canoeists. As in many locations, the canoe permits close approaches to the birds and thus provides excellent photographic opportunities. Each of these species is a summer resident, seldom recorded in the winter when the shallow streams freeze.

In the cedar-swamp water stalk two large predators of the fish—the Great Blue Heron (Photo 3-6) and the Common Egret. Both are shy and usually take flight when discovered, as does the Wood Duck. All three birds use old trees for nesting—the heron and egret make stick nests amid the limbs; the duck nests in a trunk cavity. When young Wood Ducks first emerge from the nest they must make one long jump to the ground, sometimes thirty feet below. Fortunately the downy ducklings are resilient and bounce safely.

Above the river the midges and mosquitoes are eagerly sought by three experts on the wing—the Tree Swallow, the Barn Swallow, and the Purple Martin. Only the Barn Swallow is a common breeder in the area; it nests frequently on the beams of small wooden bridges. Male and female share the two-week incubation of four or five eggs and subsequent feeding of the young. Later the male aids the fledglings while the female starts another brood. The first fledglings may help feed the second brood. Swallows are said to fly close to the ground as storms approach and, thus, warn Pine Barrens residents of bad weather. Recent research verifies this folklore: barometric pressure changes in storm fronts apparently make swallows fly lower.

PONDS

Outstanding ponds in the Pine Barrens include several at Colliers Mills, with signs at the entrance, and Lake

3-6 The Great Blue Heron. *Photograph by the author*

Oswego at Penn State Forest. Road maps clearly show the locations of these larger bodies of water. One sometimes discovers interesting birdlife on the smaller ponds scattered along the highways in the Pine Barrens.

In large depressions of the local topography, the cedar swamp waters form beautiful dark pools with emergent vegetation. Among the reeds the Redwing Blackbird, Swamp Sparrow, and Song Sparrow nest. The well-hidden nest of the Swamp Sparrow is a seldom found cup of tightly woven tussock grass. These three species remain in small numbers into the winter, until the ponds become frozen, the Song Sparrow being the most reluctant to depart.

The "hell-diver" Pied-billed Grebe attacks fish from below and the Belted Kingfisher attacks them from above. Both species were formerly blamed for reducing the number of young game fishes, but it is now known that they have little if any effect on their number. Adult kingfishers sometimes train their young on the art of fishing by setting freshly killed fishes afloat for practice dives. During migration there are also puddle ducks such as the Mallard and Black Duck on the ponds; the length of their visits depends on the extent of the hunting. I have seen these ducks become very shy the first week of the hunting season. A less common migrant at the ponds is the curious Solitary Sandpiper. Unlike most shorebirds it essentially avoids the coast, and it is the only North American sandpiper to lay its eggs in the abandoned tree nests of other birds such as the Robin.

Cedar Swamps

Cedar bogs can be explored along the nature trails of several State parks and forests, including the well-marked paths at Bass River Park and Wharton State Park. Trail

*maps are available at the park offices. Roads in Lebanon
State Forest pass through several cedar bogs.*

The rivers and ponds are surrounded by wet cedar
forests, with boglike floors. These cedar swamps provide a
unique habitat for several unusual birds. The golden Prothonotary Warbler nests in the old trees of such swamps,
and it is most easily located by its loud calls. The Parula
Warbler builds nests where *Usnea* lichen is common. The
warbler's preference for the lichen as nesting material is
remarkable—it will fly as far as a mile to secure the *Usnea*.
In the densely wooded swamps the Hooded Warbler can
sometimes be found. Again it is best to be familiar with
the bird's voice, which has a clear musical quality that easily
permeates the swamp. This thicket species can be found
most easily toward dusk when males begin to sing in the
tree-tops.

The commoner breeding birds include the American
Redstart where maples are dominant and the White-eyed
Vireo at the swamp's edge. The loud call of the vireo
always brings to mind its humorous transcription in words,
"quick, peel me an orange, quick"! It is certainly a characteristic sound of the Pine Barrens—elsewhere the species is
simply a rare migrant.

Few other generalizations of the birdlife there can be
made. Little ornithological study of the cedar swamps has
been done, and adventurous fieldwork could easily make
significant contributions. For example, the swamps may
soon be found to contain the only nesting population of
Swainson's Warbler in New Jersey—the birds have been
heard there during several recent breeding seasons.

CHAPTER FOUR

The Institute Woods of Princeton

The Institute Woods is the property of the Institute for Advanced Study, Princeton. Albert Einstein started the tradition among the resident scholars of walking in the woods for relaxation, and it is now a favorite haunt of bird watchers. Dominant trees include the beech (*Fagus grandifolia*) and several species of oak with an undergrowth of dogwood (*Cornus*). Sizeable stands of birch (*Betula*) and of aspen (*Populus*) add diversity to the younger areas of the forest. Ground plants include such notables as the moccasin flower orchid (*Cypripedium*) and several club mosses (*Lycopodium*); spring beauty (*Claytonia virginica*) and trout lily (*Erythronium americanum*) are abundant in spring.

Bordering the Institute Woods (Photo 4-1) are several habitats of note: (1) two areas of mature planted pines, (2) the Delaware and Raritan Canal and its floodplain, and (3) the Princeton Wildlife Refuge. This adjacent refuge is low and contains wet forest and open marsh. The water has been maintained at a high level to benefit nesting Wood Ducks, Prothonotary Warblers, and other swamp species. In two years I have seen 130 species of birds at the Institute Woods and adjacent refuge. A total of 180 species has been reported, and a rather high proportion of this total (about half) consists of nesters.

4-1 The Institute Woods has several miles of trails that include all parts of the forest. *Photograph by the author*

The Woods

The Institute Woods is entered most easily from the eastern boundary of the Institute for Advanced Study, just south of Princeton off Route 583 on Olden Lane. A parking lot at the end of Olden Lane has a sign marking a gravel path that leads to the woods. Enter the forest trails (all are good for bird-watching) that go left from this main path.

Of the forest birds, Woodcocks are among the first to begin spring courtship. On moonlight nights in late March the males can be heard on their spiraling flights, which end with a whirling sixty-foot dive to the ground and an abrupt landing. Between courtship flights the males walk about the display grounds giving their distinctive nasal "peeent" call. The female is attracted by the activity and selects a mate. The female then nests and raises four young, with no assistance from the male. The same courtship grounds are used year after year by successive generations of Woodcocks—I have seen the same local display ground active for more than ten years.

As soon as winter flocks begin to disperse, the Mourning Dove starts nesting. It can feed its young early in the year because of the production of "pigeon milk" in its crop. In appearance and nutritious content the milk resembles that of mammals and is regurgitated to feed the young. When nesting is completed doves begin communal roosts and in the fall adhere closely to the flock.

Both the Yellow-billed and Black-billed cuckoos are in the woods, but they are not numerous. They are usually heard, or seen briefly, on straight-line flights through the vegetation. When they do perch within sight they are often motionless and not easily detected unless they repeat their call. Both species migrate from a great distance, wintering entirely in South America. Unlike other cuckoos throughout the world, these species rarely lay their eggs in the nests of other birds.

The Yellow-shafted Flicker, Hairy Woodpecker, and Downy Woodpecker all commonly nest in the woods. Each uses a natural cavity in a dead tree or makes one in early spring. The excavation of such cavities is a real undertaking for a pair of woodpeckers—Audubon noted that the little Downy Woodpecker will work industriously for a week to construct its nesting site. Flickers generally depart in winter, but the smaller species are permanent residents. In spring my ornithology students observe the courtship of the flicker with its elaborate bowing and loud calling. The male and female face each other on a large limb and exchange bows before performing the involved courtship dance with exaggerated wing, tail, and body movements. Both maintain a careful balance. Field research has shown that the courtship inter-actions are dependent on the male's black "mustache"—it is *the* mark that identifies the sex for the birds themselves. Part of the research included painting a black facial stripe on a female, which was then treated by other birds as a male.

The Great-crested Flycatcher also nests in the woods, using old woodpecker cavities. The nest consists of many materials, including snakeskins (or, more recently, bits of cellophane). The Eastern Phoebe and Eastern Wood Pewee are also common nesting residents. The pewee's clear whis-tle is in marked contrast to the rasping whistle of the Phoebe, and the songs are one of the easiest ways to dis-tinguish the two species. The pewee will quickly come to investigate an imitation of its notes or at least respond with a call. In early June the female constructs a small lichen-covered nest, complete with three white-and-brown speck-led eggs.

A number of noisy birds follow. The Blue Jay and Common Crow are particularly evident when they surround and attack local hawks or owls. The birds apparently mob predators to drive them from the locality; this is undoubtedly beneficial, since the nocturnal Great Horned Owl will sometimes snatch a roosting jay or crow. Bird watchers use the mobbing behavior to find interesting birds: recently when I followed some noisy crows they led me to an annoyed Long-eared Owl.

Both the Carolina and Black-capped chickadees breed in the woods; in New Jersey their ranges overlap only in the central portion of the State. Because their plumages are almost the same, they are identified for certain by their calls—the more southerly Carolina Chickadee has higher and faster notes. Occasionally a single bird gives the call of both species—those who do this are probably hybrids. The closely related Tufted Titmouse is as noisy as the chickadee when it forages in small groups; the constant calling helps to keep the birds together. Their vocabulary is quite varied, and many a beginning bird watcher will trace an unknown song back to a titmouse. The White-breasted Nuthatch has a comparatively loud voice that carries far through the woods (Photo 4-2). Again the constant calling seems important in maintaining bonds between foraging birds. The White-breasted Nuthatch is one of the few species of small birds who keep the same mate for life. As with the chickadees and nuthatches, the House Wren depends on abandoned woodpecker holes for nesting. Curiously, the male House Wren often builds several nests during courtship, and the female then selects the one that will be used. The alert pair resists any nesting invasion by the Brown-headed Cowbird—the wrens break and discard the unwelcome cowbird egg. Few species show such discrimination.

4-2   The lively White-breasted Nuthatch. *Photograph by G. Ronald Austing from National Audubon Society*

The next three songsters are closely related, all members of the Mimidae, and it takes some practice to distinguish their songs. The Mockingbird is all the more difficult to identify because of its excellent imitations of neighboring species. Fortunately the Catbird inserts its characteristic "meow" call with regularity. And the Brown Thrasher usually organizes its phrases in doublets, but it can be misleading when it fails to do so. There are an additional twenty-nine species of the family Mimidae, all found in the Americas, and most are renowned for their songs.

Three members of the thrush family, Turdidae, are common nesting species in the woods—the Robin, Wood Thrush, and Veery. The Robin frequently forages on fields and lawns adjacent to the forest, while the other species remain in the woods. It is difficult to think of the ecological separation of the Wood Thrush and Veery, but the latter may be more closely associated with wet areas. The Wood Thrush is the third most common nesting species at the Institute property, outnumbered slightly by the Blue Jay and Rufous-sided Towhee. Wood Thrushes characteristically forage among the mayapples and other herbaceous growth of the forest floor, but early territorial songs are often sounded from conspicuous perches in the trees. When alarmed, the birds raise their crown feathers and utter sharp "pit, pit, pit" notes.

Both the Golden-crowned and Ruby-crowned kinglets can be seen hovering about branch tips for tiny insects, but only the Golden-crowned Kinglet is common in winter months, and neither breeds in the Institute Woods. The female Golden-crowned Kinglet may lay as many as eleven eggs per brood, their total weight being greater than the bird itself; usually one egg is laid a day. Except for the hummingbird, the kinglets are the smallest birds of eastern North America.

The Starling is regularly seen moving through the forests, but it seems to prefer life in nearby suburban yards. Considering its high-pitched notes, it is not surprising that the Starling's hearing range covers much higher frequencies than the range of the human ear. This has led some communities to use ultrasonic noises in attempts to drive the starlings away. The attempts have not been very successful, but the idea has more merit than other noise-making schemes. The common Red-eyed Vireo differs from the Starling in its softer voice and preference for the deep forest. The abandoned nests of both species are sometimes adopted as homes by arboreal mice.

Warblers are numerous; in fact, the Institute Woods may have more species than any similar-sized area in the State. A number of southern rarities are regularly found there in the spring, with some outstanding breeding records. The common warblers include the American Redstart in the forest and the Blue-winged Warbler near the early successional stages of scrub and thickets. The Kentucky Warbler remains an uncommon nesting bird, perhaps because it is approaching the northernmost region of its breeding (southern New York). The bird builds a delicate domed nest of leaf litter on the forest floor, a nest that entirely hides the incubating adult. On occasion I have been startled when a Kentucky Warbler rapidly flew out of a hidden nest only a few feet from where I was standing. The bird then perched nearby and scolded with sharp notes. Another groundnesting warbler is the very common Ovenbird, so named for its domed grass nest that looks like a tiny Dutch oven. In the wetter areas of the marsh at Princeton Wildlife Refuge, the Yellow Warbler and Yellow-

throat are evident in summer. The Chestnut-sided Warbler
is also a common nesting resident and an excellent predator
of caterpillars; its diet includes both the fuzzy gypsy moth
and the tent caterpillar.

During migration a host of other warblers frequent the
forest for brief visits; these include the Tennessee Warbler,
Nashville Warbler, Magnolia Warbler, Black-throated Blue
Warbler, Blackburnian Warbler, Blackpoll, Canada Warbler,
and others. At the peaks of migration it is a most exciting
area; on a good May morning one may find up to twenty-
five species in this family. In this their breeding season the
birds are conspicuous for their bright plumage and frequent
songs. To tally many species it is essential to know their
calls—I review a bird record before a May walk. Unfortunately older bird watchers often have difficulty hearing
the high-pitched songs of warblers. For example, many are
unable to hear the thin voice of the Blackpoll, whose entire
call is above 8,000 cycles a second.

Within the forest Baltimore Orioles usually nest near
wet areas. It is still not known why urban orioles attach
their nests to tree limbs that overhang streets. During nest
construction the birds eagerly accept short pieces of yarn
that can be offered by leaving them on a nearby shrub. The
complicated pendulous nest of the Baltimore Oriole reflects
an antipredator adaptation common to many orioles in the
tropics. Its construction makes the nest inaccessible to egg-
eating snakes or mammals. Common Grackles are close relatives of the orioles and are also among the breeding birds
of the forest. In spring and fall they are abundant in noisy
migration flocks that invade nearby fields for fallen corn
or other grain. The Grackle's strong jaw muscles and seed-
cracking keel in the middle of the bill equip him for cracking kernels. Brown-headed Cowbirds are very common in

the forest, where they deposit their eggs in the nests of a variety of other birds. The most recent writings on cowbirds suggest that this parasitic habit arose through necessity, when the birds followed great bison herds that were constantly on the move and allowed them no time to stop for nesting. A second theory holds that parasitism originated when the cowbirds sometimes produced eggs before their own nests were built and laid them in the nests of other birds. Neither theory has been evaluated by field studies, but the former seems more reasonable.

In late spring the Scarlet Tanager returns from South America to breed at the Institute Woods. The species is especially appreciated by those New Jersey residents who recognize it as one of the strongest predators of the gypsy moth. It has been recorded as consuming more than thirty-five tiny caterpillars a minute.

The Rufous-sided Towhee and Rose-breasted Grosbeak are the most common breeding members of the finch family, Fringillidae. Both nest in the forest; the Towhee usually down low, however, while the grosbeak is up high. It is a surprise to discover that the male grosbeak bursts forth in full song while incubating in the nest. Unfortunately the grosbeaks put little effort into nest building, and their eggs or young are often lost in windstorms. In appropriate habitats several sparrows breed—near wet and shrubby areas the Swamp and Song sparrows and near open areas the Chipping and Field sparrows. Common winter finches include the Slate-colored Junco, Tree Sparrow, and White-throated Sparrow. During migration Fox Sparrows pass through quickly; I have counted as many as thirty in a day. The Fox Sparrow is certainly one of the most attractive sparrows, and it ranges over most of North America (the western ones are much darker than the eastern). It is usually discovered scratching in the leaves of the forest floor with White-throated Sparrows. The interesting "double scratch" method of feeding is practiced by many finches— it involves a very rapid backward kick with both feet simultaneously, to remove as much of the leaf litter as possible. While kicking, the bird hops slightly to maintain its upright posture. Some sparrow species have not mastered this efficient technique and still forage by scratching the ground with one foot. Young birds require a certain maturity before they can effectively "double scratch" as the adults do.

CHAPTER FIVE

Hutcheson Memorial Forest Property

The William L. Hutcheson Memorial Forest property (which includes adjacent fields) is a natural research area of Rutgers University. The land is open to the public only for scheduled tours, which are conducted throughout the year. Information on tours is available from the Department of Botany, Rutgers College, New Brunswick. The forest is located on Amwell Road, just east of East Millstone.

The William L. Hutcheson Memorial Forest consists of sixty-three acres of mature oak woods, representing part of the only virgin land in New Jersey. This land is owned by Rutgers University and is used primarily as a natural research reserve. Inasmuch as the forest has been uncut since 1700 it provides a unique climax habitat, and it is of considerable interest to ecologists. The birds of the forest have been studied under long-term banding projects initiated by Jeff Swinebroad and continued by Rutgers students and myself.

Surrounding the forest is a large set of fields, most of them 1 hectare each, the date of whose last plowing is known. This set of fields provides a direct look at succession in natural vegetation (Photo 5-1). Plants of the first year after cultivation is stopped include common ragweed (*Ambrosia artemisiifolia*), lamb's quarters (*Chenopodium album*), wild radish (*Raphanus raphanistrum*), three-seeded mercury (*Acalypha rhomboidea*), and yellow wood sorrel (*Oxalis stricta*). As the fields remain uncultivated there is a regular change of plant species through invasion of seeds dispersed by wind or birds. Early invading trees include the dogwood, red maple, red cedar, and the introduced tree of heaven (*Ailanthus altissima*). The fields are usually dominated in the early stage by broom sedge (*Andropogon*) as well. A forest of saplings may appear in thirty years and a young woodland in fifty years. Cultivated fields with such crops as soybeans, alfalfa, and corn also are maintained on or near the forest property.

FIELDS

The most common predator is the Sparrow Hawk, often seen hovering above the open fields. While hovering it has the ability to remain stationary above a possible prey by carefully co-ordinating its flight speed with the wind. If a brief search is unproductive, the hawk continues with a forward flight. Although it forages for grasshoppers or meadow voles, it nests at the edge of the forest in a hollow tree trunk, often in the top of a broken oak. It is quite adaptable and will eagerly accept as a nest a box from any farmer who wishes to control mice. The young Sparrow Hawk makes awkward sallies on its initial flights from the nest cavity and feeds on insects until it acquires the hunting skills of the adults.

Field game includes the Pheasant, Bobwhite, and Mourning Dove (Photo 5-2). The Pheasant seems a worthy

5-1 The fields of the Hutcheson Memorial property surround the forest itself, in the background. This field is three years old. *Photograph by the author*

5-2 The Mourning Dove. *Photograph by Karl H. Maslowski from National Audubon Society*

meal, but the dove, with its fast flight, is a challenging target for hunters. Good game management is necessary for hunting the Bobwhite—the hunters can remove half of a local population in a single season. How much better it is to hear the birds calling every day! In the colonial period Bobwhite Quails were extensively hunted for food and sold for as little as a penny apiece. Of course, hunting is not allowed on the research property.

Swallows of several species forage over the fields, especially during the late summer. Most numerous are the Barn and Tree swallows, over cultivated and uncultivated fields alike. Both species are masters of the air, remaining in flight while feeding, drinking from the stream, or even when preening.

The Bluebird is no longer common, for reasons not yet known, but the Hutcheson fields provide one of the few remaining locales for the species in nesting season. The actual nest is in a hollow stump. The Bluebird forages in the fields, but even there its appearance has become intermittent, and the species' future is uncertain. Biologists have suggested several possible causes of the birds' scarceness, including competition with the introduced Starling for nesting holes and the widespread use of pesticides.

Recently plowed portions of the property attract numbers of Robins, which bring the seeds of forest plants in their crops, such as seeds from dogwood berries. This is another species that has suffered from insecticides applied to lawns and shade trees. The toxic chemicals are washed into the ground by rain and mixed with soil that is eaten by earthworms. The birds then accumulate the poisons through their earthworm diet. I have seen many Robins dying from such poisoning—they characteristically lie on their backs, with wings trembling and feet oustretched in a *rigor mortis* position. Whenever one sees many birds being killed in this way he should immediately notify the State's Department of Environmental Protection.

Bands of transient Water Pipits appear briefly in late autumn, having traveled hundreds of miles from the arctic tundra. They pass through the fields quickly on their way to coastal wintering grounds. Later, as winter snow begins to dust the fields, Horned Larks are common. This is the only lark native to North America and it is representative of a worldwide family of seventy-five species. One foreign member of the family, the European Skylark, which is famous for its elaborate aerial songs, was introduced in New York City before the turn of the century, but none survived. A few Horned Larks remain to nest in the Hutcheson fields in early spring. The open nest is a simple depression on bare ground, so eggs or young are often lost in late snow or hail storms.

Where sufficient pasture is available Meadowlarks nest and attract attention by calling from fence posts or sometimes even from the top of telephone poles. As with many birds of the pasture, the ground-nesting Meadowlarks suffer considerable mortality when nesting coincides with the mowing season. Farmers regret this loss as much as bird watchers because these birds are excellent predators of grasshoppers. Because Meadowlarks are polygamous the females alone are responsible for building the domed grass nests, incubating the clutch, and raising their three to seven nestlings apiece. The males finally assume some responsibility after the young fledge and the females start second nestings.

Blackbirds are the most numerous field visitors, migrating in tremendous flocks in spring and fall. In such numbers they can cause serious loss to growers of corn and other grains. Redwings and Common Grackles arrive literally in the thousands. Various controls include the traditional scarecrow and the more modern noise-cannon, which makes an explosive blast every twenty minutes. I think the poisoned-grain techniques of recent years are rather unsuccessful and potentially dangerous. The grackle, Meadowlark, and Redwing are but a few of the many species in the blackbird family, Icteridae. More than ninety species occur in this New World group, from Alaska to Tierra del Fuego.

The Indigo Bunting is probably best considered a forest-edge species, but is certainly a common forager of weed seeds or insects of the field. As with many birds, the male returns in spring a few days earlier than the female to establish its territory. Joining it is the American Goldfinch (Photo 5-3), which is especially fond of the thistle—in fact, thistle seeds quickly attract goldfinches to feeding stations. This finch is sometimes called the "wild canary" and is well known to bird watchers for its confusing color-changes through the seasons. It is the official State bird of New Jersey as well as of Iowa and Washington.

Other sparrows breeding in these fields include the Grasshopper Sparrow, which is especially partial to old grassy upland meadows. This diminutive bird is named for its curious call, a brief insectlike trill. The disappearance of upland meadows throughout New Jersey has been accompanied by a decline in the number of Grasshopper Sparrows, so that many beginning bird watchers are unfamiliar with their interesting song. Likewise, the Vesper Sparrow of farm fields has drastically declined, although one may still hear it at Hutcheson. Fortunately, Chipping Sparrows and Field Sparrows remain common as summer breeding birds. Both use the young low cedars of the fields for their nests and are easily followed through the nesting

5-3 The American Goldfinch, State bird of New Jersey. Here the male brings food to the incubating female. *Photograph by G. Ronald Austing from National Audubon Society*

cycle. Song Sparrows also frequent the older fields, and in winter certain forest finches forage the fields in flocks, especially Slate-colored Juncos and White-throated Sparrows.

Fields throughout other parts of the State provide the only breeding habitats for a number of its scarcer birds, such as the Upland Plover, Bobolink, and Henslow's Sparrow. Some natural fields must be saved—not just State forests.

Agricultural fields also remain to be studied in detail; only the important game or pest birds are being researched. One area likely to provide new information on bird biology consists of New Jersey sod-farms, where accidental or rare migrants, such as the Buff-breasted Sandpiper and Golden Plover, are apparently regular transients.

CHAPTER SIX

Johnson Park,
New Brunswick

Most city parks have only very simple vegetation, but scattered clumps of trees and shrubbery can attract a surprising variety of birdlife. Further, if there are ponds in the park the diversity can be remarkable—Central Park, in the heart of New York City, is visited each year by more than two hundred species of birds, few of whom nest, however, because of the habitat limitations and human activity. Parks can thus provide an interesting area for local bird study (Photo 6-1), especially in migration seasons. In most parks, one encounters a fair number of bird watchers, and the companionship or exchange of information is often welcome.

Johnson Park is a narrow 600-acre strip along the north shore of the Raritan River floodplain. The park presents many recreational opportunities, such as tennis, skating, fishing, a trotting track, picnic groves, and athletic fields. For nature lovers the Park Commission has foresightedly provided the Renwick Bird Sanctuary and other natural areas. There the Raritan is still fresh water but subject to tidal influences from the Raritan Bay.

Along the undisturbed sections of the bank, canary grass

6-1 A family of Canada Geese on a park pond. *Photograph by the author*

(*Phalaris arundinacea*) dominates. Pasture grass (*Agrostis*) and a number of goldenrods flourish away from the river where fields remain. Shrubs and vines include the widespread species of *Rubus* and *Rhus,* such as poison ivy. The prevalence of common trees is associated with a natural moisture gradient from the river to upland sites. These are river birch (*Betula nigra*), slippery and American elm (*Ulmus*), tulip tree (*Liriodendron tulipifera*), white ash (*Fraxinus americana*), oaks, and maples. However, the greatest part of the park consists of open lawn.

About one hundred and fifty species of birds have been recorded at Johnson Park, and future additions are expected. The nesting list is impressive, with fifty-seven species, forty of which breed within the forest strip. Unfortunately, some of the park is threatened by highway developments, a common danger to the limited open spaces of all urban areas.

PONDS AND THE RIVER

Johnson Park lies along the northern shore of the Raritan River in New Brunswick. Entrances to the park are along River Road and from Landing Lane. Water birds are most readily found along the river east of Landing Lane.

During their post-breeding wanderings in the heart of late summer, several species of herons visit the park. Most commonly the Green Heron squawks from the river bank; sometimes it visits the park ponds to catch introduced goldfish. The species is rather intolerant of approach by others of its kind—a Green Heron that lands close to another is likely to be attacked. The only other heron that regularly feeds in the Raritan at this point is the Little Blue Heron. The herons congregate in groups where low water has left minnows stranded in small shallow pools. The white juveniles, more commonly seen than the blue adults, resemble egrets, so one should be cautious in identification. A few Great Blue Herons are recorded, but they seldom remain in the park, because they tend to avoid people. These majestic birds live for about fifteen years; it is probable that the same ones visit the park each year.

The wild waterfowl have mixed somewhat with the domestic ducks of the park, but wild Canada Geese, Mallards, and Black Ducks are evident on the river. The all-white domestic ducks are introductions from an Oriental breed, the Peking Duck. Hybrids from matings of wild and domestic ducks typically show a mixture of plumage patterns from both parents. All three of the wild species nest there, and the elaborate courtship of the ducks can be easily studied in early spring. Typically, pairing ducks exhibit a complicated series of distinctive gestures that have been descriptively named by animal behaviorists as head-pumping, tail-shaking, wing-stretch, and so forth. Most sequences rapidly culminate in actual mating if the female is receptive; otherwise she simply swims away. Sometimes there is strong competition for mates; courting males become aggressive toward each other and vigorously pursue the females. The variety of displays of courting ducks in early spring can be enjoyed at almost any small duck pond throughout the State.

The Spotted Sandpiper is the only nesting shorebird at the park (Photo 6-2). It nests from May to July, laying its four eggs on high stony patches, to avoid tidal flooding. In the fall it loses its spotted plumage and departs for the winter in South America. Common migrants include the Killdeer, which may breed nearby, the Woodcock, which is found in the woods, both the Greater and Lesser yellow-

6-2 The Spotted Sandpiper. *Photograph by Donald S. Heintzelman*

legs, the Least and Semipalmated sandpipers. The last four shorebirds are strictly migrants in this portion of the Raritan, most often found foraging along the river edge at low tide when the mud flats are exposed. As the tide rises the migrants are pushed closer to the river banks until, eventually, high water causes them to take flight and resume their journey.

Gulls also share the river, their numbers at the park shifting hourly according to the tide. They are present all year, but the greatest number appear in winter. Because most of the gulls breed far north of New Jersey, the summer gulls of the park are nonbreeding adolescents. Herring Gulls and Ringbilled Gulls are the most common, although the Great Blackbacked Gull has been conspicuously increasing in number in recent years. This aggressive bird is clearly dominant over the smaller gulls and is able to take food from them. The daily schedule of all the gulls seems to include some distant foraging, from which they usually return in the late afternoon. They may venture to the Raritan Bay salt marsh or a Perth Amboy landfill for garbage. The closely related Forster's Terns are prevalent at the park as they forage up the river with the tides. This species nests a few miles to the east of the park on some remanent salt marshes and is apparently tolerant of polluted estuaries. The Forster's Tern is probably misidentified more than any other bird at the park—the white in the wings is the key field mark to distinguish it from the Common Tern. In the early fall young terns join the adults in forays along the Raritan.

The river also attracts swallows, which pass back and forth foraging for insects. Both the Rough-winged and Barn swallows nest on beams under the major bridges, which is remarkable in view of the heavy traffic, day and night. Both species are long-distance migrants, passing far into Central and South America during the winter months and returning to New Jersey as early as April. As with many species that feed while in flight, they migrate during the daylight hours, in contrast to many ground feeders that are nocturnal migrants. The mud cup-nest of the Barn Swallow requires hundreds of parental flights for its construction—adults make seemingly endless trips to a mud puddle for successive billfuls of mud. The nest is eventually lined with soft grasses, and it serves two broods, of four nestlings each, a year.

Park Woods and Lawn

Land birds at Johnson Park are most abundant in the parkland and woods west of Landing Lane. There are several trails through the area, including a Bird Sanctuary path with an entrance sign beside the west picnic grove.

Numerous hawks have been recorded as they passed overhead, including groups of migrating Broad-winged Hawks, but none can really be considered common. As will be noted later, most migrating hawks pass along mountain ridges such as are found in northwestern New Jersey. In fact the only nesting predators seem to be the owls. Screech Owls (Photo 6-3) undoubtedly enjoy the abundance of white-footed mice in the river forest, and Great Horned Owls still nest. there, feeding on squirrels and other rodents and rabbits In the metropolitan areas of the State Screech Owls control rodents in parks and are encouraged with nesting boxes or even with introduced pairs. Barn Owls also frequent city parks if a nesting site such as an open steeple is available nearby.

Pigeons are present at the park but are less common

6-3 The Common Screech Owl, recently renamed the Northern Screech Owl, since it has many tropical relatives. *Photograph by Allan D. Cruickshank from National Audubon Society*

than in the city itself. Pigeon colors are highly variable, reflecting former selective breeding in captivity, but the wild pattern of the ancestral Rock Dove from Europe still dominates. This original pattern consists of a dark neck and breast, and gray wings with two prominent black stripes. Park pigeons are usually far less healthy than wild doves because of the amount of unnutritious food they are fed, such as popcorn. Mourning Doves nest low in the small trees of the park or, more rarely, on the ground. Most frequently I find their flimsy stick nests in planted evergreens, which probably provide more protection than open deciduous trees.

Yellow-shafted Flickers are common in open areas during the summer months, feeding on the lawns. During courtship the males often hammer on buildings or metallic drain pipes with their stout bills. The extra loud sound produced by the resonant substrate undoubtedly increases a male's chance of attracting a mate. Downy Woodpeckers are also common at the park and breed in the wooded sections. Their courtship drumming is amplified by the use of a hard, hollow tree limb.

The most common flycatcher is the Eastern Kingbird, which eats only insects during the summer months. It makes frequent sallies from a hunting perch as the insects fly by. Some of the maneuvers used in catching insects with erratic flight are spectacular—the kingbird uses its winged expertise with precision. In fall, the bird increases the amount of berries in its diet, and, with fewer insects in cooler weather, it may depend chiefly on fruit. Oddly, the kingbird seizes berries much as it does live insects, by plucking them in flight. The Great-crested Flycatcher (Photo 6-4) and Eastern Wood Pewee breed in the woods and are easily distinguished by their calls. The pure whistled call of the

6-4 The Great Crested Flycatcher, the State's largest forest fly-catcher. *Photograph by Donald S. Heintzelman*

pewee is one of the first daybreak sounds, while the raspy whistle of the Great-crested Flycatcher can be heard even at noon. The lichen-covered nest of the pewee is so well disguised that it is difficult to find unless one carefully follows an adult bird. Both the Common Crow and Blue Jay are nesting residents, obvious throughout the day and quick to snatch picnic leftovers. The jays also exploit the heavy acorn crops of the oaks in fall and bury many of the seeds for winter use. Black-capped Chickadees and Tufted Titmice are permanent nesting residents in the woodlots, flocking together during their continual foraging. The southern titmouse seems to be more sensitive than the chickadee to harsh weather conditions in winter; the titmouse seeks calm and sunny areas for foraging. Field studies have shown that both must capture an "average food item" every ten seconds to survive in cold periods. The resident White-breasted Nuthatch is so common that it doubtless breeds nearby, although no nest has yet been discovered in the park. The cavity nest is usually made in old trees and most easily discovered when the nestlings are calling noisily.

House Wrens, Catbirds, and Brown Thrashers can be found in the shrubbery during the summer. The Catbird and thrasher are long-lived—they have banding records of nine and eleven years, respectively. In contrast the smaller wren has only a five-year maximum. As a general correlation, small size is related to short life because of the very high rates of metabolism and exaggerated energy needs of small birds. This metabolic difference is reflected in all their behavior—the catbird and thrasher lead average avian lives with moderate activity and four or five young per brood, whereas the tiny wren is a flurry of activity, in constant motion with seven or eight young a nest. In more open areas the Mockingbird and Robin are common. Both species tolerate people, nesting in shrubs along the busiest paths or beside buildings. I have even seen a Robin nesting in a roadside telephone booth.

Starlings nest noisily in the trees, and in winter large roosting flocks sometimes form. These flocks can number tens or hundreds of thousands of birds in large cities and are considered an unpleasant addition to the parks. Unfortunately they are generally successful in resisting human attempts to disperse them, including chemical repellents and electrical shock systems.

Few warblers nest in the park, and of these only the Yellow and Yellowthroat are common summer residents, both near water. The Yellow Warbler's nest is often the repository of a cowbird's egg, left by the quick visit of a female cowbird with the intention that it be incubated and raised by the unsuspecting warbler. But the Yellow Warbler is usually able to detect the intruder's egg and simply starts again by building a second nest on top of the original. Many additional warbler species are easily found during migration periods, however, and morning visits to the park in the spring can be rewarding. Most likely to be found are the Parula, Magnolia, Black-and-white, Black-throated Green, Black-throated Blue, Blackpoll, and Redstart. These migrant warblers appear together in flocks that exhibit remarkable cohesion in spite of frequent fights. Other less common species are found regularly among the waves of migrants. It should be emphasized that the waves of migrants cause considerable daily variations in the number of birds—some days the warblers are conspicuous, some days there are only a few. Frequent visits to a park help to spot the exciting "highs" in migration activity. Daily weather maps from the newspapers are also useful—many birds move through after the passage of a warm front.

The House Sparrow is so common about the picnic tables that perhaps we should look up the recipe for sparrow pie, regularly served in New York City hotels at the turn of the century. About the park the sparrows have rather untidy nests of straw and string, candy wrappers and rags. The Red-winged Blackbird, Common Grackle, and Brown-headed Cowbird occur along the river forest in large mixed flocks during migration periods. A small number of grackles remain to breed in a loose summer colony. Unlike most species grackles exhibit great variation in egg colors and markings from nest to nest, an adaptation of unknown significance. The most attractive member of the blackbird family, the Baltimore Oriole, nests near the river. Its song fills the park along the river bank throughout the early summer. Its voice even seems an appropriate addition to the outdoor concerts of late May and June. The oriole's pendulous nest hangs from limbs of the tallest shade trees along the river, containing from four to six eggs or nestlings.

Other attractive nesting birds are included in the finch family—the Cardinals in low bushes, the Rose-breasted Grosbeaks in deciduous trees, and the Rufous-sided Towhees well hidden on the woodland floor. Two other finches breed in the park: the Chipping Sparrow, which is common on summer lawns, and the Song Sparrow, present all year and singing in almost every month. Common migrants include the Slate-colored Junco and the White-throated Sparrow, both of which remain through the winter, vigorously feeding on weed seeds. All of the winter sparrows benefit from the shelter of shrubbery along the park edge. The American Goldfinch is common throughout most of the year, and I have seen it feeding young in the park as late as October. Most birds feed their young a strict insect diet high in protein; the goldfinch adds partially digested seeds through regurgitation. Young birds themselves are unable to digest hard seeds directly until their crops and gizzards have developed fully. As with many birds, the juveniles beg for food from the patient adults by vibrating partially open wings and extending their necks while chirping loudly.

CHAPTER SEVEN

Great Swamp
National Wildlife Refuge

The Great Swamp National Wildlife Refuge is a wonderful tribute to the land-saving efforts of conservation-minded people in the Northeast. This 6,000-acre refuge contains an excellent fresh-water swamp and is described by the United States Department of the Interior as the "largest unspoiled area of its kind between Maine and Virginia." Ornithologically it is the most richly wooded wetlands in the State (Photo 7-1) and the most accessible National Wildlife Refuge in the nation—thirty million Americans live within an hour's drive of the Great Swamp. Manhattan, Paterson, Newark, and Elizabeth are all within a radius of twenty-five miles. Nevertheless, it took a long public battle to save this beautiful area from use as a jetport or for other developments.

The refuge has two sections established by law, a managed area and a wilderness area. There will be foot-trails in the latter half, which will otherwise be left undisturbed, as prescribed by Congress in 1968. The management unit has nature trails, an educational center, and habitats specifically modified for wildlife, such as ponds for migrant waterfowl.

7-1 The boardwalk trail through the wet forest of the Great Swamp
National Wildlife Refuge. *Photograph by the author*

In the swamp, low marshes alternate with low-lying ridges or knolls. The typical swamp plants include cattail (*Typha*), sedges (*Carex*), and a variety of shrubs, such as azalea (*Rhododendron*) and highbush blueberry. The swamp trees include willow (*Salix*), red maple, and elm. On the dryer ridges and hummocks are upland trees such as oak, beech, and birch.

The richness of the Great Swamp is reflected also in its vertebrate fauna—more than two hundred species of birds, almost half of which are nesting species, thirty species of mammals, including beaver, flying squirrel, and red fox, eight turtle species, twelve snake, at least six salamander (including New Jersey's only Blue-spotted Salamanders), one lizard, and twelve frog species.

THE FRESH-WATER SWAMP

The Great Swamp is just east of Basking Ridge, New Jersey. Maps of the refuge are available at the headquarters, indicated by signs from Basking Ridge. Two boardwalk trails are good for bird-watching—that at the Wildlife Observation Center and that at the Morris County Outdoor Education Center. Both have well-marked entrances and are about a mile long.

The two biggest fishing birds at the refuge are the Great Blue Heron and the little Green Heron (Photo 7-2). Both stay late into the fall until thin ice begins to cover the ponds. Thereafter the Great Blue Heron moves south slowly, while the Green Heron departs rapidly for the Gulf states. There are also the American Bitterns, which hide among the cattails with a plumage-camouflage that makes them quite inconspicuous, although they may be as common as the other herons. In spring the bitterns begin courtship with

7-2　A Green Heron at the edge of a small swamp. *Photograph by the author*

booming calls in the early morning, often under the shroud
of mist or fog. The unique call sounds mechanical, somewhat like a noisy water pump, and is most mysterious to
the uninitiated ear.

Migrant waterfowl make good use of the refuge; such
use was the original purpose of the National Wildlife
Refuge system. A good fall day may bring a tally of the
following: Canada Goose, Mallard, Black Duck, Gadwall,
Pintail, Green-winged Teal, Blue-Winged Teal, Shoveler,
American Widgeon, Wood Duck, and Ruddy Duck. The
teals are small ducks, usually weighing less than a pound,
with a rapid flight, up to forty miles an hour. Most exciting
of all the waterfowl is the nesting population of Wood
Ducks—certainly the largest in the State, with at least fifty
pairs (a wonderful comeback for a species that was almost
lost). Many of the Wood Ducks use nest boxes mounted on
short poles to protect themselves from raccoons. Other
nesters now include the Canada Goose, Mallard, and Black
Duck. The geese are important for the refuge's role in waterfowl production, so management includes the construction
of "wash-tub" nesting platforms in the marshes.

Birds of prey are not widely represented at the swamp,
but I have spotted Red-tailed, Broad-winged (Photo 7-3),
Marsh, and Sparrow hawks during a single afternoon. Nests
have been found of the Sparrow and Red-tailed hawks and,
less commonly, of the Red-shouldered Hawk. The latter is
characteristically a predator of the wet woodlands. It is
seen regularly with a snake in its talons, but mice provide
at least half of its diet. A nesting pair of Red-shouldered
Hawks often uses the same large stick-nest year after year
to raise two or three young.

Through careful management, particularly of food
plants, the refuge has maintained breeding populations of

7-3 An immature Broad-winged Marsh Hawk about to strike. *Photograph by G. Ronald Austing from National Audubon Society*

the three gallinaceous (chicken like) game birds: the Ruffed Grouse, Bobwhite, and Ring-necked Pheasant. The Bobwhite unfortunately continues to be scarce, possibly because of the low vitality of the stock introduced from other areas of the country. Native Bobwhites are of course better adapted to local conditions. Wild Turkeys also have been introduced but their future is uncertain because the species is easily disturbed by human activity, and they wander away from the refuge within a year of their release.

The Virginia Rail nests amid the cattails, and it is always an exciting discovery. The Virginia Rail and the Sora (Photo 7-4) are most often seen in the early morning or on a cloudy day along the edges of the marsh. In summer both species are strictly "walkers," seldom seen in flight, and yet they make long migrations to the West Indies and Central America in the fall.

Migrant shorebirds are not common, but a late August visit to a dried pond can yield a few species, including the Killdeer and Spotted Sandpipers that nest there in summer. In the wooded sections of the refuge the Woodcock produces its fuzzy young. The discovery of a new Woodcock family is intriguing—the adult bobs up and down in a display of alarm while the downy young disperse in all directions.

As in other areas, the Mourning Dove continues to increase in numbers, and I believe this is related to the mildness of recent winters. The Mourning Doves are the only native species that can drink water directly. They immerse their bills in the refuge ponds and imbibe in this position; other birds must tilt the head upward and use gravity to swallow water. Doves have a muscular throat for drinking in this manner, much as a horse has.

The two species of cuckoos are common breeders, and

7-4   The Sora is the most common member of the elusive rail family. *Photograph by Donald S. Heintzelman*

both are recognized as important predators of a variety of harmful caterpillars. Owl censuses at the refuge have been surprising in recent years. There have been estimates of a dozen Great Horned Owls and fifty Screech Owls. Night counts are conducted in the early spring when the calling owls can be easily tallied. The Barred Owl is a bird of the river floodplain and the owl most easily attracted by an imitated call—even in daytime human hoots can attract this bird. I have called a Barred Owl out of a swamp to a perch within twenty feet of me, which startled both of us. The Screech Owl also responds to an imitation of its call, even if it is not very accurate. Apparently owls that have territories are quick to respond to any possible intrusion by another owl of the same species.

Chimney Swifts feed over the ponds, especially at dusk, flying at a maximum speed of seventy miles an hour. For many years the erratic flight of swifts was attributed to a unique alternation in wing beats, but slow motion photography proved that the wings move in unison; the illusion is caused by the swift's rapid alternate bending of the entire body from left to right. Their diet is strongly affected by seasonal changes in the supply of insects. In fact, late spring cold spells can cause mortality among the nestlings by reducing the number of insects available to them, although young swifts can adjust to brief food shortages by becoming torpid. They temporarily lower their body temperature and reduce their energy needs.

The Belted Kingfisher dives for fish throughout the day, unless strong winds make the water too rough to see the fishes clearly. Unfortunately, its numbers there reflect a decline in New Jersey. One factor that limits the number of kingfishers is that they require an exposed sandy bank into which they can dig a six-foot nesting burrow. Sometimes they are shot when they repeatedly visit the fish hatcheries of northern New Jersey.

Nesting woodpeckers are well represented. In order of abundance they are the Downy Woodpecker, Yellow-shafted Flicker, Hairy Woodpecker, Red-bellied Woodpecker, Pileated Woodpecker, and Red-headed Woodpecker. The Hairy and Downy are named for the texture of their respective plumage, the Downy being somewhat smaller and softer. The flicker is well named for its bright wing feathers, in contrast to the inappropriately named Red-bellied Woodpecker, which has barely a tint of rose on its gray underparts. The Red-headed Woodpecker has a bright red head as an adult and is often considered one of America's most beautiful birds. Because the young of this species entirely lack the red, they were misidentified as a new species by early American ornithologists. The Pileated Woodpecker is named for its red crest (*pileus* means cap) and is otherwise known as the "Logcock" in backwoods country. In flight it resembles a crow but has bold white patches on its wings.

The flycatcher family, Tyrannidae, is also well represented by breeding species. Again, in order of abundance they are the Eastern Wood Pewee, Great-crested Flycatcher, Eastern Phoebe, Traill's Flycatcher, and Least Flycatcher. The Acadian Flycatcher from the south is expanding its range and will probably return to the refuge; its numbers greatly decreased in this region about the turn of the century. The species is misnamed, for the specimen from the south was confused with a bird found in Canada and hence named as a northern or "Acadian" species. The confusion is understandable as the small flycatchers are difficult to identify. However, the voices of the different species are quite distinct and most useful for the bird watcher. Undoubtedly, the songs are the most important feature in selecting a mate of the same species. Field experiments show that flycatchers are unable to distinguish between different species by appearance alone.

In the managed area Tree Swallows benefit from nest boxes, while Barn Swallows help themselves to buildings not necessarily made for them. Both species gather in sizeable fall flocks before departing for the winter. These flocks often assemble along highways, and in early cold spells the birds may huddle together for warmth. Year-round residents include the Blue Jay, Common Crow, Black-capped Chickadee, Tufted Titmouse, and White-breasted Nuthatch.

Three kinds of wrens nest regularly at the refuge: the House Wren (Photo 7-5) in upland scrub and nest boxes, the Carolina Wren in forest thickets, and the Long-billed Marsh Wren among the cattails around ponds. Recent fieldwork at the refuge suggests it also contains, along the grassy edges of the marsh, some of the few nesting Short-billed Marsh Wrens in the State. Proof of breeding will require some effort because the grass nests are well hidden and males often build nonfunctional nests.

Mockingbirds, Catbirds, and Brown Thrashers are all common. An unprecedented number of these birds have stayed over during recent mild winters, but they migrate south in harsh years. Young birds appear to be more variable in their migration movements than the adults, which return to the refuge year after year.

These are four nesting thrushes: the uncommon Bluebird in open areas, the Robin about the headquarters, the Wood Thrush (Photo 7-6) in the areas with tall trees, and the Veery in the swamp woods. The ground nest of the Veery is often very close to the water, and it is strange that it does not lose more young to water snakes. During

7-5 The House Wren was pictured by Audubon nesting in an old hat; here it uses a gourd house. *Photograph by Allan D. Cruickshank from National Audubon Society*

7-6 The Wood Thrush, one of the State's most abundant forest birds. *Photograph by A. W. Ambler from National Audubon Society*

migrations the Hermit and Swainson's thrushes are common in the wooded areas. Unfortunately, the beautiful songs of these birds are usually accompanied by the unpleasant hum of mosquitoes at the swamp. Mosquitoes can transmit avian malaria and encephalitis to the warm-blooded birds.

Among the most abundant birds at the refuge are the Starling, which nests in tree holes, and the Red-eyed Vireo, which builds a beautiful little cup-nest of tightly woven fibers. I have noticed that the Vireo, unlike the Starling, often forages in quiet pairs prior to nesting. Other common breeders are found among the warblers: Black-and-white (woods), Blue-winged (field edges), Yellow (willows), Chestnut-sided (thickets in open area), Yellowthroat (wet thickets), and the Redstart (woods). Curiously, few migrant warblers are reported to be common at the refuge, but no one could miss the hundreds of Myrtle Warblers that flock through in fall and spring, some of which remain throughout the winter. In summer the Myrtle Warblers go as far north as trees are found, to breed in small evergreens.

The House Sparrow and Redwing are also common nesters, and during migration periods the Redwings become abundant. As with most species, well over half of each fall Redwing flock consists of the juveniles born that summer. Meadowlarks invade the fields in summer and provide continuous song during courtship. The recent invasion of nesting Redwings in the fields has undoubtedly caused competitive pressures between these two species. In summer Baltimore Orioles are common, but only the colorful males are conspicuous, as the females are dull-colored and, until July, incubating at the nest. Flocks of Common Grackles and Brown-headed Cowbirds also abound, with little animosity between species. The courting behavior of these two birds is rather elaborate, with bows, mutual preening, and aggressive chases. One should be able to notice the displays in March and April. Courting cowbirds seem un-discriminating—I recently watched two males go through full displays together, and captive birds will even display to humans.

In the forest the Scarlet Tanager and Rose-breasted Grosbeak, with their Robinlike voices, seem equally common. Again, only the males of these species are colorful; the females are protectively dull colored. This plumage difference greatly affects the numbers of sightings—I usually see about four males for every female, although the sex ratio is nearly one to one. Both species center their activities in moist forests, while Cardinals frequent the edge of dryer woods. Unlike other drab females, the feminine Cardinal is conspicuous in that she has a song that rivals her mate's voice, which is rarely the case among birds. A few of the upland pastures attract field finches such as the American Goldfinch, Chipping Sparrow, and Field Sparrow. But the Song Sparrows and Swamp Sparrows of the widespread wet areas are really much more representative of the Great Swamp.

CHAPTER EIGHT

High Point State Park and Stokes State Forest

More than twenty-three thousand acres of the north-western corner of New Jersey are preserved in these two adjacent State properties. This region of the Kittatinny Mountains contains the highest elevation in the State (maximum 1,803 feet) and fortunately is in fairly undisturbed condition.

In most of the park chestnut oaks (*Quercus prinus*) dominate, with an undergrowth of ericaceous shrubs. The trees of this forest include, beside the chestnut oak, red oak (*Quercus rubra*), and red maple. Important shrubs are blueberries and huckleberries (*Gaylussacia*). In broad valleys, oak-hardwoods invade, while rocky ridge-tops sprout pitch pine and scrub oak. Cooler ravines shelter northern conifers, such as hemlock and firs.

Cedar swamps (Photo 8-1) provide a favorable habitat for a number of species of breeding birds. Major trees of the swamps are oak, hemlock, birch, and gum, as well as the white cedar itself. *Chamaecyparis thyoides*. A rich sphagnum-moss mat covers the floor.

Small ponds in the area are often formed by beaver dams. Other natural lakes have been made by glaciers. Until

8-1 The edge of a bog at Kuser Natural Area, High Point State Park. *Photograph by the author*

recent surveys of breeding birds were conducted, the north-west corner of New Jersey had been the least studied area in the State ornithologically. Still, with more than two hundred species recorded in the area, much remains to be learned about the seasonal distribution of birds in this northern boundary of high elevation.

MOUNTAIN RIDGE TOPS

The Kittatinny Mountain ridge is most accessible from Route 206 as it goes northwest through Stokes State Forest. Just past Culvers Lake a sign points to a park road leading directly to the ridge top, at Sunrise Mountain, about four miles away. The mountain lookout south of the parking lot is excellent for hawk-watching.

The exposed ridges of the Kittatinny Mountains parallel the Delaware River through both the State park and forest. The easternmost ridge has beautiful viewpoints to the southeast (Photo 8-2). In early fall particularly, the vantage points allow one to see hundreds of birds of prey in a single day as they glide south on the thermal updrafts at the ridges. I would recommend Sunrise Mountain at Stokes or Racoon Ridge near the Delaware Water Gap for such hawk-watching—both are excellent areas and beautiful with autumn foliage. These lookouts are on the Appalachian Trail, and I find it most enjoyable to pack a lunch for a day of hiking and hawk-watching. On the fall afternoons of the weekend many hawk watchers gather at the lookouts—it can be a social affair as well as an outing.

In mid-September, when the conditions are favorable, with northwest winds, hundreds of Broad-winged Hawks pass along each day. As the most abundant hawk, the Broad-winged Hawk remains through the end of the month; 10,000

8-2 A view from Sunrise Mountain in Stokes State Forest, Sussex County. *Photograph by the author*

were tallied in the early fall of 1972. This species travels in small circling flocks, known to bird watchers as "kettles." They have a long migration, wintering far into Central and South America. On this four-thousand-mile trip they avoid any passages over water as they are greatly dependent on thermals for gliding.

Another early fall migrant is the endangered Osprey. Formerly I used to count up to sixty a day, but now a season's total may be less than a hundred. Its decline in number is unfortunately paralleled by that of several other predatory birds of the hawk ridges. It seems somewhat out of place along the inland mountains as it is otherwise a coastal species in New Jersey, but its range covers much of North America wherever there are lakes or large rivers.

Toward the beginning of October there are many Sharp-shinned Hawks and a lesser number of their larger relative, the Cooper's Hawk. Good daily counts for these species are fifty and four, respectively. Both species show a marked sexual dimorphism in size—the females are much larger than their mates. This is a common feature in many hawks throughout the world and probably reduces food competition between the sexes, the males taking smaller prey than the females. This interesting morphological difference can cause identification problems since a female Sharp-shinned Hawk may be almost as large as a small male Cooper's Hawk; hence, one should be cautious of size as a means of identification.

At the end of October the beautiful Red-tailed Hawk is the dominant species, yielding November counts of up to a thousand a day. With the crisp fall winds the Red-tailed Hawk often circles the lookouts and displays its distinctive rusty tail. As with many species of buteos—soaring hawks with broad wings—this bird can vary considerably in color, from a dark chestnut on the breast to an almost pure cream. Unfortunately the Red-tailed Hawk, although protected by law, is still shot by those who are unaware of its rodent diet. Other birds of prey that can be recorded easily during the fall movements include the Turkey Vulture, Red-shouldered Hawk, Marsh Hawk, and Sparrow Hawk. Migrating birds of prey sometimes make playful attacks or passes at other hawks as they travel along the ridge. These aerial encounters reveal the hawk's maneuverability at its best— a circling Broad-winged Hawk will dive at a Red-tailed Hawk, or a Marsh Hawk will pursue its own kind. Each of these species is easily identified by means of field guides, although the Red-shouldered Hawk in flight may resemble the Broad-winged Hawk except for the white wing patches of the former. Six other hawks and falcons are recorded each fall, but they are rare species. These are the Bald Eagle, Peregrine Falcon, Pigeon Hawk, Goshawk, Golden Eagle, and Rough-legged Hawk. Concentrations of other small migrants, notably thrushes and warblers, also move along the ridges, but it is the great hawk flights that attract Kittatinny Mountain bird watchers. Many of the smaller birds migrating along the mountain seem occupied with their journey and rather oblivious to human observers—for example, a White-breasted Nuthatch once flew right into me in its haste.

FOREST

There are many excellent forest trails through High Point State Park and Stokes State Forest. These foot trails are marked from their roadside entrances, and together they offer many miles of hiking. Detailed trail maps are available at both State offices—on Route 206 and on Route 23 in the preserves.

Spring in the deep weeds brings the courtship drumming of Ruffed Grouse (Photo 8-3) and the evening flights of Woodcocks. Both are popular game birds in the area and are fairly elusive. In winter the grouse may be tracked by their foot prints with feather-marks in the snow, or by pellets of digested buds. In more open woods Mourning Doves are common in summer, but few remain through the harsh winters of this part of the State. The northern doves also seem to have two broods annually, rather than three or four as elsewhere in New Jersey.

Woodpeckers are more diverse here than in any other region, with the Sapsucker, Flicker, and four other woodpeckers—Hairy, Downy, Red-headed, and Pileated. The last two species are making their final stand there, seldom breeding elsewhere in the State. The Red-headed Woodpecker was more common formerly, but it had the unfortunate habit of flying low across roads or feeding on roadside insects; the advent of automobiles made this habit potentially lethal for the birds. Even now I occasionally see one dip through traffic. The Pileated Woodpecker seems to have a better future: it is beginning to tolerate human activities and may actually be expanding its range with the aid of feeding stations. Sighting one of these giants is still an event, however, whether the bird is drilling a feeding hole or simply flying overhead. In searching for the Pileated Woodpecker bird watchers listen for its extra-loud "flicker" call or look for the characteristic rectangular feeding holes, often drilled near the base of trees. A month after the young woodpeckers hatch they leave the nesting chamber, and the large cavity is used by owls or any of a variety of mammals.

Nesting flycatchers include the Great-crested Flycatcher, Eastern Pewee, Phoebe, Eastern Kingbird, and

8-3 The Ruffed Grouse. Photograph by Charlie Ott from National Audubon Society

Least Flycatcher. The Great-crested Flycatcher and Pewee usually remain well within the deciduous forests and are more often heard than seen. The Least Flycatcher prefers nesting in open woods, where one may hear its sharp "chebec" call. It is primarily a northern species, known only as a migrant in southern New Jersey. Given favorable conditions, the energetic bird raises two broods a year in the same nest. Near bridges the Phoebe is evident (its nests are often placed under bridges on the support beams) and active, usually feeding on insects flying above the water. As the Phoebe waits for insects from its stream-side perch it incessantly wags its tail up and down, perhaps as an aid in balancing. In the most open places, the Eastern Kingbird is the dominant flycatcher. Like other members of the tribe, the kingbird is insectivorous in summer, eating a great variety of insects from butterflies to wasps. It will even dine on honeybees from their hives, and this habit has considerably reduced its popularity with farmers. The kingbird is sometimes reported to attract the insects it eats by raising the reddish crown patch of its head, but this idea seems far-fetched as the insect eye is not very receptive to red light. It is more likely that the patch is raised in aggressive displays between kingbirds.

The common members of the Corvidae family in northwestern New Jersey are the Blue Jay and Common Crow. The Raven is a rare migrant there, although it breeds in the mountains of nearby states. Distantly related to the crows, Black-capped Chickadees, Tufted Titmice, and White-breasted Nuthatches are also common in the forest as permanent nesting residents. However, the titmouse is a southern species that has recently expanded its range; it has been in the Stokes area for only about thirty years. Like many insectivorous birds, the titmouse seems to benefit from the additional food available in years of heavy insect infestation in the forest.

From the thickets, House Wrens call with a loud bubbling song. They are one of the most aggressive species in defense of their nests, chasing away much larger birds that stray too close to the nesting cavity. The Brown Thrasher can also be found in the shrubs from May through October. In northern New Jersey this low-nesting species sometimes loses eggs to the predatory black snakes that are common on the mountain ridges. John James Audubon's plate of the Brown Thrasher shows several birds fighting a black snake that is invading a nest, albeit the battle seems lost. Birds sometimes repel or even kill predatory snakes by pecking directly at the eyes.

Farther into the forest, the Wood Thrush and Veery are evident, at least in breeding season, when their flutelike calls make an early morning walk rewarding. I usually hear the spring Wood Thrush a full week before the Veery, but by the end of May both species are in full song, even in the cooler parts of the State.

The two kinglets are migrants in this region. The Golden-crowned remains through the winter, however, while the Ruby-crowned continues farther south. Recently some Golden-crowned Kinglets have remained into summer in conifer plantations along the northern border of New Jersey; a few nest there.

In the 1960s the Starling invaded the northwestern woodlands, where it now seems to be abundant. The Red-eyed Vireo and Black-and-white Warbler are also quite common in the forest, although the Vireo has apparently declined in numbers in recent years. Some current research suggests that this decline may be related to the control programs for the gypsy moth, since the aerial sprays (chemicals such as Sevin etc.) may reduce other insects of the forest canopy that serve as food for the bird. Of course if stronger pesticides are used there may be a direct toxic effect on the birds as well. Other insectivores include the Ovenbird, the Yellow Warbler, and both the Blue-winged and Golden-winged warblers. The House Sparrow also has invaded this forest area, as it has all parts of the State. Only since 1955, however, has it invaded the cooler mountain ridges. The Brown-headed Cowbird may be similarly expanding into the deep forest, at the expense of the Wood Thrush, whose nests it frequently utilizes. Censuses reveal that as many as half of the Wood Thrush nests may be parasitized by a cowbird egg—a condition that dramatically reduces the thrush reproduction.

New Jersey's only common tanager, the Scarlet Tanager, reaches its greatest abundance in this corner of the State. The drab green female blends in with the forest vegetation; the bold red-and-black plumage of the breeding male is in striking contrast. In fall the male molts and assumes green plumage too, and both sexes depart for the winter in South America. In their winter area they must compete with numerous other tanagers, as more than two hundred species of the family, Thraupidae, reside in the tropics of the New World. With such competition it is not surprising that the Scarlet Tanager often loses considerable weight before spring.

The finch family includes the Cardinal, another species that spread from the south and reached the high ridges only in the late 1950s. I predict that a series of harsh winters may eliminate them from this cold area in future years. There too the Rufous-sided Towhees scratch the forest leaf litter in search of insect grubs and larvae. In the rhododendron thickets of the Stokes forest one can usually hear a towhee scratching through the leaves before one glimpses the bird itself. In this rich forest the feeding efficiency of the species is much greater than in poorer areas such as the Pine Barrens; hence the feeding territories of the northern birds can be correspondingly smaller. The low nest is defended vigorously by the nesting female—she will remain to dispell and distract any intruder, even people within a few feet.

Smaller finches include the Slate-colored Junco, which comes in numbers from the north in winter. It is suspected that this species may also breed in this part of New Jersey, as a few of its young have been observed at Stokes in July. Another winter resident is the common Tree Sparrow, which departs in early April as the Chipping Sparrow arrives from the south for the summer. The White-throated Sparrow is considered a winter visitor throughout New Jersey, but it too may breed in small numbers in this cool northwest section. In its more northern haunts it prefers to nest among evergreens or in areas recently burned by forest fires. The Song Sparrow, which is a permanent resident throughout the State, may emigrate from this high area in severe winters.

CEDAR SWAMPS

An outstanding cedar swamp is located at the northern boundary of High Point State Park. Follow park signs north from Route 23 to the John D. Kuser Natural Area, which has a trail encircling the bog. The trail begins directly from the Natural Area parking lot.

More than thirty species of birds breed in the beautiful highland swamps, including a number of northern species that breed nowhere else in the State (for example, the Magnolia Warbler). The most common nesting birds of this habitat are familiar to everyone—the Catbird and Robin. After these, certain warblers are most numerous, including the ubiquitous Redstart and Yellowthroat, and two species which nest only in the highest elevations of New Jersey at Stokes—the Northern Waterthrush and Canada Warbler. Future fieldwork will undoubtedly turn up several new breeding species in the State. Unfortunately, it is really quite difficult to work through the interior of these swamps because the boglike substrate makes walking difficult.

Ponds and Lakes

The most profitable lake for bird-watching in this region is Culvers Lake, just north of Route 206 at the entrance to Stokes State Forest. The lake is indicated by signs, and highway maps show the road that can be used to explore it. The causeway at the northern end and the Lake's outlet at the southern end are recommended areas.

Waterfowl are not common in the region, but both the Black Duck and Wood Duck nest there. The Black Ducks' chicks can be seen along most pond edges in late May, while the young Wood Ducks appear by mid-June. The latter particularly frequent beaver ponds in the Stokes forest, which contain an abundance of dead trees for nesting cavities. Of the migrant ducks, the Common Merganser is probably the most prevalent, at least in the spring. Canada Geese are common overhead in migration, but few flocks rest on the mountain ponds (Photo 8-4). Along the pond shores the Spotted Sandpiper nervously bobs; it raises its brood between mid-May and mid-July. There is some dispute about the function of the sandpiper's bobbing but it

8-4 Lake Wapalanne in the northwest corner of New Jersey. *Photograph by the author*

seems related to vision and the search for food—the movement may permit it to see deeper.

In ponds where fish are present one can expect to find the Belted Kingfisher. The species is unusual among birds, for the female is more colorful than the male (only females have the deep chestnut breast bands). Also feeding at the ponds are two aerial insect feeders—the Chimney Swift and the Tree Swallow. Both species forage for hours over the water, and both use old woodpecker holes in trees at the ponds for their nests. Like most of the birds closely associated with the ponds, the swift and swallow depart in the fall, before early frosts bring the first thin layer of ice.

PART II

Records of
New Jersey Birds

CHAPTER NINE

The Seasonality of New Jersey's Birds

Like those of other temperate areas, New Jersey's avifauna exhibits pronounced seasonal patterns of activity and abundance. Migrations are the most obvious movements, extending from late February to late May, when the peak occurs, and from late July to November, with the peak in early October. Irregular flights within a season are not migrations but are important as seasonal changes with irregular departures (finches), post-breeding dispersal (herons), and winter wanderings. Also, as ponds freeze in winter waterfowl must migrate temporarily south to open water (Photo 9-1). In a review of the avian year, I have constructed a four-part calendar and classified each species as a permanent resident, winter resident, spring and fall transient, or summer resident. It should be obvious that not every species easily fits into one of these categories, but the system is useful for a good overall view of the seasonal elements in the State's bird life. The calendar provides also a general guide to when each species may be found in the State and a fairly definite breeding period. A species varies in its dates of occurrence more widely than in its dates of breeding.

9-1 A Pied-billed Grebe. This bird retreats to the south as ponds freeze. *Photograph by the author*

TABLE 9-1

Seasonal Composition of the Avifauna in Cape May County, N.J.
Number of Species Present Each Month for Each Group

	Jan.	Feb.	Mar.	Apr.	May	Jun.	Jul.	Aug.	Sep.	Oct.	Nov.	Dec.
Permanent Residents	45	45	45	45	45	45	45	45	45	45	45	45
Transients	9	8	17	29	49	21	25	55	67	60	39	32
Summer Residents	9	5	13	34	66	64	66	70	76	47	22	16
Winter Residents	42	41	36	31	18	10	12	10	25	38	41	46
Total no. Species	105	99	111	139	178	140	148	180	213	190	147	139

Data extracted from Witmer Stone's *Bird Studies at Old Cape May: An Ornithology of Coastal New Jersey*, rev. ed., 2 vols. (New York, 1965). Note how a few summer residents are present as stragglers in the winter months and a few winter residents remain into the summer.

Three hundred species are included in these tables, yielding 47 permanent residents (16%), 116 summer residents (39%), 65 transients (21%), and 72 winter residents (24%). Of the 181 nesting species, 46 are permanent residents and 110 are summer residents; the rest are uncommon breeders. A seasonal summary is shown of the changes in the composition of bird life throughout the year at Cape May, where Witmer Stone did an excellent monthly analysis of bird life.

A brief index of the seasonal changes in activity can also be obtained by a tabulation of the total number of species *breeding* each month (of course most birds would be represented in more than one month).

TABLE 9-2

Total Number of Species Nesting Each Month in New Jersey

Jan.	Feb.	Mar.	Apr.	May	Jun.	Jul.	Aug.	Sep.	Oct.	Nov.	Dec.
1	2	10	53	150	172	126	41	4	—	—	—

A similar table can be compiled for the occurrence of common species throughout the year. No rare or unusual birds are included; the chart is concerned with the dominant species:

TABLE 9-3

Number of Common Species in New Jersey for Each Month

Jan.	Feb.	Mar.	Apr.	May	Jun.	Jul.	Aug.	Sep.	Oct.	Nov.	Dec.
77	80	96	142	152	122	124	131	136	134	97	77

It is clear that May is the bird watcher's busiest month, but every season has variety, with its own characteristic species.

Breeding Periods of Permanent Residents

GROUP [1]	SPECIES	BREEDING PERIODS
Waterfowl	Mute Swan	March–May
	Mallard	March–July
	Black Duck	March–July
	Gadwall	May–June
Birds of Prey	Turkey Vulture	April–June
	Red-tailed Hawk	March–May
	Marsh Hawk	May–June
	Sparrow Hawk	April–July
Pheasant and Quail	Ruffed Grouse	April–June
	Bobwhite	May–August
	Ring-necked Pheasant	April–July
	American Coot	May–June
Gull	Herring Gull	June–July
Dove	Mourning Dove	March–September
Owls	Barn Own	March–August
	Screech Owl	April–May
	Great-horned Owl	January–April
	Barred Owl	March–May
	Long-eared Owl	April–June
Woodpeckers	Pileated Woodpecker	May
	Red-bellied Woodpecker	April–June
	Red-headed Woodpecker	May–July
	Hairy Woodpecker	April–May
	Downy Woodpecker	April–May
Perching Birds	Blue Jay	April–June
	Common Crow	May–June
	Fish Crow	April–June
	Black-capped Chickadee	May–June

[1] The groups used here are natural categories familiar to most bird watchers rather than formal taxonomic groups; they parallel standard orders and families.

Breeding Periods of Permanent Residents (*Continued*)

GROUP	SPECIES	BREEDING PERIODS
Perching Birds (cont'd.)	Carolina Chickadee	April–June
	Tufted Titmouse	May–June
	White-breasted Nuthatch	April–May
	Carolina Wren	April–July
	Mockingbird	April–July
	Cedar Waxwing	June–September
	Starling	March–August
	House Sparrow	April–August
	Eastern Meadowlark	May–August
	Red-winged Blackbird	May–August
	Boat-tailed Grackle	May–July
	Common Grackle	April–June
	Brow-headed Cowbird	May–July
	Cardinal	April–August
	House Finch	June–July
	American Goldfinch	July–September
	Song Sparrow	April–August

Migration Dates for Winter Residents

GROUP	SPECIES	ARRIVES	DEPARTS
Loons	Common Loon	October	May
	Red-throated Loon	October	May
Grebes	Red-necked Grebe	March	April
	Horned Grebe	October	April
Gannet	Gannet	August	May
Cormorants	Great Cormorant	October	March
	Double-crested Cormorant	September	May
Waterfowl	Whistling Swan	October	April
	Brant	October	April

Migration Dates for Winter Residents (*Continued*)

GROUP	SPECIES	ARRIVES	DEPARTS
	Snow Goose	October	April
	Blue Goose	October	April
	Pintail	October	May
	*Green-winged Teal	September	April
	*American Widgeon	September	May
	Redhead	October	April
	Ring-necked Duck	October	April
	Canvasback	December	March
	Greater Scaup	November	April
	Lesser Scaup	November	April
	Common Goldeneye	October	April
	Bufflehead	October	April
	Oldsquaw	November	April
	Common Eider	December	March
	King Eider	December	March
	White-winged Scoter	September	April
	Surf Scoter	September	April
	Common Scoter	September	April
	*Ruddy Duck	October	May
	Hooded Merganser	October	April
	Common Merganser	October	April
	Red-breasted Merganser	November	April
Birds of Prey	Rough-legged Hawk	October	May
	*Bald Eagle	September	April
Shorebirds	*Common Snipe	September	May
	Purple Sandpiper	November	May
	Dunlin	October	April
	Sanderling	July	May
Gulls	Glaucous Gull	November	March
	Iceland Gull	November	March
	*Great Black-backed Gull	September	May

* Species which have been recorded as nesting in New Jersey.

Migration Dates for Winter Residents (*Continued*)

GROUP	SPECIES	ARRIVES	DEPARTS
Gulls (cont'd.)	Ring-billed Gull	September	May
	Bonaparte's Gull	October	May
	Black-legged Kittiwake	November	February
Auks	Razorbill	November	February
	Dovekie	November	February
Owls	Snowy Owl	November	March
	Short-eared Owl	September	March
	Saw-whet Owl	October	May
Perching Birds	*Horned Lark	September	June
	Boreal Chickadee	December	March
	*Red-breasted Nuthatch	September	May
	*Brown Creeper	September	April
	*Winter Wren	September	April
	*Golden-crowned Kinglet	October	April
	Ruby-crowned Kinglet	October	April
	Northern Shrike	October	March
	Myrtle Warbler	September	May
	Rusty Blackbird	October	May
	*Evening Grosbeak	October	May
	*Purple Finch	October	May
	Pine Grosbeak	November	March
	Common Redpoll	December	March
	Pine Siskin	October	April
	*Red Crossbill	November	May
	White-winged Crossbill	November	April
	Ipswich Sparrow	November	March
	*Slate-colored Junco	October	April
	Tree Sparrow	October	April
	White-crowned Sparrow	October	May
	*White-throated Sparrow	September	April
	Fox Sparrow	November	April
	Lapland Longspur	November	April
	Snow Bunting	November	March

Migration Dates for Transient Species

GROUP	SPECIES	SPRING	FALL
Waterfowl	*Blue-winged Teal	March–May	September–October
	*Shoveler	March–April	October–November
Birds of Prey	* Goshawk	—	October–November
	*Sharp-shinned Hawk	—	September–November
	*Cooper's Hawk	—	October
	Golden Eagle	—	November
	Peregrine Falcon	—	September–October
	Pigeon Hawk	—	September–November
Shorebirds	Semipalmated Plover	April–June	July–October
	American Golden Plover	—	August–November
	Black-bellied Plover	May	August–October
	Ruddy Turnstone	May–June	August–October
	Whimbrel	April–May	August–September
	Solitary Sandpiper	April–May	August–September
	Greater Yellowlegs	April–May	August–November
	Lesser Yellowlegs	April–May	July–October
	Knot	May	August–October
	White-rumped Sandpiper	May–June	August–October
	Baird's Sandpiper	May–June	July–September
	Least Sandpiper	May	July–September
	Short-billed Dowitcher	May	July–August
	Long-billed Dowitcher	—	October–November
	Stilt Sandpiper	—	August–October
	Semipalmated Sandpiper	May	July–October
	Western Sandpiper	—	July–October
	Buff-breasted Sandpiper	—	July–September
	Marbled Godwit	—	August–October
	Hudsonian Godwit	—	August–October
	*American Avocet	—	August–October
	*Black-necked Stilt	—	August

Migration Dates for Transient Species (*Continued*)

GROUP	SPECIES	SPRING	FALL
Shorebirds	Red Phalarope	—	August–November
(cont'd.)	Wilson's Phalarope	—	August–October
	Northern Phalarope	—	August–October
	Parasitic Jaeger	—	September–October
Terns	Caspian Tern	May	August–October
	Black Tern	—	July–September
Woodpecker	Yellow-bellied		
	Sapsucker	April–May	September-October
Perching	Western Kingbird	—	September–November
Birds	Yellow-bellied		
	Flycatcher	May–June	September
	Olive-sided Flycatcher	May	August–September
	*Common Raven	—	October–December
	Swainson's Thrush	May	September–October
	Gray-cheeked Thrush	May	September–October
	Loggerhead Shrike	May	September
	*Solitary Vireo	May	October
	Philadelphia Vireo	May	September
	Tennessee Warbler	May	August–September
	Orange-crowned		
	Warbler	—	October–December
	*Nashville Warbler	May	September
	*Parula Warbler	May	September
	*Magnolia Warbler	May	September
	Cape May Warbler	May	September–October
	*Black-throated Blue		
	Warbler	May	September
	*Blackburnian Warbler	May	September
	*Yellow-throated		
	Warbler	May	—
	Bay-breasted Warbler	May	September
	Blackpoll Warbler	May	September
	Palm Warbler	April	October
	*Northern Waterthrush	May	August–September

Migration Dates for Transient Species (*Continued*)

GROUP	SPECIES	SPRING	FALL
	Connecticut Warbler	May	September–October
	Mourning Warbler	May–June	September–October
	Wilson's Warbler	June	August–September
	Dickcissel	—	October–December
	Lark Sparrow	—	September–November
	Lincoln's Sparrow	March–April	October–November

Migration and Breeding Dates of Summer Residents

GROUP	SPECIES	ARRIVES	DEPARTS	BREEDING DATES
Grebe	*Pied-billed Gebe	March	November	April–June
Shearwaters	Cory's Shearwater	June	September	—
	Greater Shearwater	June	October	—
	Sooty Shearwater	May	June	—
Petrels	Leach's Petrel	May	October	—
	Wilson's Petrel	May	October	—
Herons	*Great Blue Heron	March	November	April–July
	*Green Heron	April	October	May–July
	*Little Blue Heron	April	October	May–August
	*Cattle Egret	April	October	June–August
	*Common Egret	April	October	April–August
	*Snowy Egret	April	October	April–August
	*Louisiana Heron	April	September	May–August
	*Black-crowned Night Heron	March	November	April–June
	*Yellow-crowned Night Heron	April	October	April–July
Bitterns	*Least Bittern	April	September	May–July
	*American Bittern	April	October	May–July
Ibis	*Glossy Ibis	April	October	June–July
Waterfowl	*Canada Goose	February	November	April–June
	*Wood Duck	March	September	April–July

Migration and Breeding Dates of Summer Residents (*Continued*)

GROUP	SPECIES	ARRIVES	DEPARTS	BREEDING DATES
Birds of Prey	*Broad-winged Hawk	April	October	April–June
	*Osprey	March	October	May–August
Rails	*King Rail	April	November	May–July
	*Clapper Rail	April	October	May–August
	*Virginia Rail	April	October	May–July
	*Sora	April	November	May–July
	*Black Rail	May	October	June–July
Shorebirds	*Common Gallinule	April	October	May–September
	*American Oystercatcher	April	September	June
	*Piping Plover	March	September	May–July
	*Killdeer	March	October	April–July
	*American Woodcock	February	December	March–June
	*Upland Plover	April	September	May–July
	*Spotted Sandpiper	April	September	May–July
	*Willet	April	October	May–July
Gulls and Terns	*Laughing Gull	March	November	June–July
	*Gull-billed Tern	April	September	June–July
	*Forster's Tern	April	November	June–July
	*Common Tern	April	October	June–August
	*Roseate Tern	May	October	June–July
	*Least Tern	May	September	June–July
	Royal Tern	May	October	—
	*Black Skimmer	May	September	June–September
Cuckoos	*Yellow-billed Cuckoo	April	October	May–August
	*Black-billed Cuckoo	April	October	May–August
Nighthawks	*Chuck-will's-widow	April	October	May
	*Whip-poor-will	May	September	May–June
	*Common Nighthawk	May	September	May–June
Swift	*Chimney Swift	April	September	June
Hummingbird	*Ruby-throated Hummingbird	May	October	June–July
Kingfisher	*Belted Kingfisher	April	October	May–July
Woodpecker	*Yellow-shafted Flicker	March	October	May–July

Migration and Breeding Dates of Summer Residents (*Continued*)

GROUP	SPECIES	ARRIVES	DEPARTS	BREEDING DATES
Flycatchers	°Eastern Kingbird	May	September	June–August
	°Great Crested Flycatcher	May	August	May–July
	°Eastern Phoebe	March	October	April–July
	°Acadian Flycatcher	May	September	June–July
	°Traill's Flycatcher	May	September	June–July
	°Least Flycatcher	May	September	May–July
	°Eastern Wood Pewee	May	September	June–July
Swallows	°Tree Swallow	April	October	April–June
	°Bank Swallow	April	August	May–July
	°Rough-winged Swallow	March	August	May–July
	°Barn Swallow	May	September	May–August
	°Cliff Swallow	April	September	May–July
	°Purple Martin	April	September	May–August
Wrens	°House Wren	April	October	May–July
	°Long-billed Marsh Wren	May	September	May–August
	°Short-billed Marsh Wren	April	October	May–August
Mimics	°Catbird	April	October	May–August
	°Brown Thrasher	April	October	May–July
Thrushes	°Wood Thrush	May	October	May–July
	°Hermit Thrush	April	November	May–July
	°Veery	May	October	May–August
	°Eastern Bluebird	March	November	April–July
Gnatcatcher	°Blue-gray Gnatcatcher	April	October	April–June
Vireos	°White-eyed Vireo	April	November	May–July
	°Yellow-throated Vireo	May	September	May–June
	°Red-eyed Vireo	May	October	May–August
	°Warbling Vireo	April	September	May–June
Warblers	°Black-and-White Warbler	April	September	May–June

Migration and Breeding Dates of Summer Residents (*Continued*)

GROUP	SPECIES	ARRIVES	DEPARTS	BREEDING DATES
Warblers (cont'd.)	°Prothonotary Warbler	May	August	June
	°Worm-eating Warbler	May	September	June
	°Golden-winged Warbler	May	August	May–June
	°Blue-winged Warbler	May	August	May–June
	°Yellow Warbler	May	August	May–June
	°Black-throated Green Warbler	May	September	June–July
	°Cerulean Warbler	May	September	May–June
	°Chestnut-sided Warbler	May	October	June–July
	°Pine Warbler	April	October	May
	°Prairie Warbler	May	September	June–July
	°Ovenbird	May	September	May–July
	°Louisiana Waterthrush	May	September	May–July
	°Kentucky Warbler	May	September	May–July
	°Yellowthroat	May	October	May–July
	°Yellow-breasted Chat	May	September	June–July
	°Hooded Warbler	May	August	June–July
	°Canada Warbler	May	September	June–July
	°American Redstart	May	September	May–July
Blackbirds and Orioles	°Bobolink	May	September	May–June
	°Orchard Oriole	May	September	May–July
	°Baltimore Oriole	May	September	May–June
Tanagers	°Scarlet Tanager	May	September	May–July
	°Summer Tanager	April	August	June–July
Finches	°Rose-breasted Grosbeak	April	October	May–July
	°Blue Grosbeak	May	October	June–July
	°Indigo Bunting	May	September	May–August
	°Rufous-sided Towhee	April	November	May–August
	°Savannah Sparrow	March	November	May–July
	°Grasshopper Sparrow	May	October	May–July
	°Henslow's Sparrow	May	October	May–July

Migration and Breeding Dates of Summer Residents (*Continued*)

GROUP	SPECIES	ARRIVES	DEPARTS	BREEDING DATES
	*Sharp-tailed Sparrow	April	October	May–August
	*Seaside Sparrow	May	October	May–August
	*Vesper Sparrow	April	November	May–July
	*Chipping Sparrow	April	October	May–August
	*Field Sparrow	April	October	May–August
	*Swamp Sparrow	April	October	May–July

CHAPTER TEN

The Christmas Bird Counts and Big Day Counts in New Jersey

Part 1. *Christmas Counts.* It was once the custom to go hunting on Christmas day and shoot as many birds as possible, or at least a good potful. At the beginning of the century the National Audubon Society sought to change this custom into the sport of bird-watching—getting people to hike and observe as many birds as possible during one day. The sport took hold, and today more than twenty thousand participants engage in the annual activity. The rules are fairly simple: (1) count numbers and species of all birds seen during the day, (2) use a "count area" of not more than fifteen miles in diameter, and (3) send reports to the Audubon Society. The counting areas (more than a thousand in North America) are established by former censuses; a map shows recent counting centers in New Jersey (Map 3). A list of the actual counts and names of the party leaders is also presented in *American Birds* magazine to help any reader who wishes to engage in this exciting pastime; a count takes just one day of a two-week period around Christmas. It provides an invigorating experi-

MAP 3 The distribution of Christmas Counts for New Jersey in 1971–72. Each dot shows a Count center. The oldest Christmas Count area (Princeton) is marked with an arrow. The Cape May Count area, marked with a star, records the greatest number of species each year.

TABLE 10-1

The Most Abundant Species (Average Yearly Count)

Species	Average No. a Year
1. Starling	85,812
2. Herring Gull	64,085
3. Common Crow	50,132
4. Brant	24,659 *
5. Dunlin	21,773
6. House Sparrow	16,748
7. Redwing Blackbird	15,351
8. Black Duck	15,183
9. Mourning Dove	11,984
10. Slate-colored Junco	10,909
11. Mallard	9,567
12. Blue Jay	7,834

Data from 1970–71 and 1971–72 New Jersey Counts.
* Brants vary greatly in numbers; there was a serious decrease from 1969 to 1973.

ence shared with other bird watchers in the same counting area.

Actual numbers of species are presented for four recent years in the following Christmas count review. One interesting point should be emphasized—amid the great diversity of species only a few dominate numerically, as listed in Table 10-1.

In 1971–72 almost one-fourth of all the birds tallied were Starlings; the top ten species accounted for two-thirds of the overall total; and twenty species provided more than four-fifths of the total. In other words, the real numbers of any count are contributed by a very small proportion of abundant species—an important ecological principle. The Christmas Counts are also useful in considering population trends as shown in Table 10-2.

TABLE 10-2

Some Population Trends Shown by Christmas Counts
in New Jersey from 1969–73.

	Population Changes			
	1967–70	1970–71	1971–72	1972–73
Decrease because of some biological factor				
Brant (74% decrease)	40,422	28,854	20,463	10,583
Increase by changes in wintering area:				
Snow Goose (172% increase)	2,471	3,410	5,785	6,727
Decreases of northern birds in mild winters				
Horned Lark (53% decrease)	2,474	2,110	1,185	1,161
Tree Sparrow (58% decrease)	7,549	4,712	4,593	3,181
Snow Bunting (90% decrease)	867	536	143	89
Increases of southern birds in mild winters				
Ruddy Turnstone (185% increase)	47	67	132	134
Carolina Wren (63% increase)	127	152	163	207

TABLE 10-3

A Four-Year Summary of Christmas Counts in New Jersey
(Highest counts of the four-year period are italicized)

GROUP	SPECIES	*1969–70*	*1970–71*	*1971–72*	*1972–73*
Loons	Common Loon	19	*89*	56	39
	Red-throated Loon	358	*392*	54	205

TABLE 10-3 (*Continued*)

GROUP	SPECIES	1969–70	1970–71	1971–72	1972–73
Grebes	Red-necked Grebe	—	3	—	—
	Horned Grebe	156	502	221	358
	Pied-billed Grebe	85	685	139	127
Gannet	Gannet	3	3	180	60
Cormorants	Great Cormorant	24	4	20	27
	Double-crested Cormorant	15	8	3	6
Herons	Great Blue Heron	210	280	265	292
	Green Heron	—	4	1	3
	Little Blue Heron	87	53	96	29
	Cattle Egret	2	—	—	—
	Common Egret	14	76	22	115
	Snowy Egret	136	173	342	78
	Louisiana Heron	16	9	46	13
	Black-crowned Night Heron	206	139	193	203
	Yellow-crowned Night Heron	12	1	—	—
Bittern	American Bittern	2	25	29	21
Ibis	Glossy Ibis	—	4	23	17
Waterfowl	Mute Swan	211	130	456	435
	Whistling Swan	32	148	161	153
	Canada Goose	4,402	3,922	6,954	4,887
	Brant	40,422	28,854	20,463	10,583
	Snow Goose	2,471	3,410	5,785	6,727
	Blue Goose	3	2	5	6
	Mallard	6,801	9,643	9,491	10,028
	Black Duck	22,993	15,188	15,178	23,625
	Gadwall	114	179	184	306
	Pintail	866	400	941	263
	Common Teal	—	—	1	1
	Green-winged Teal	599	487	1,162	437
	Blue-winged Teal	—	1	26	3
	European Widgeon	2	1	1	1
	American Widgeon	1,171	3,518	1,305	779
	Shoveler	462	515	874	544

TABLE 10-3 (*Continued*)

GROUP	SPECIES	*1969–70*	*1970–71*	*1971–72*	*1972–73*
	Wood Duck	13	*43*	39	23
	Redhead	17	79	20	*138*
	Ring-necked Duck	158	*349*	182	138
	Canvasback	4,991	3,459	1,844	8,568
	Greater Scaup	9,310	*28,553*	8,707	6,903
	Lesser Scaup	640	820	*1,065*	256
	Tufted Duck	—	—	1	—
	Common Goldeneye	535	*1,987*	525	873
	Bufflehead	3,910	*7,531*	2,864	2,517
	Oldsquaw	2,567	*3,571*	1,677	3,284
	Harlequin Duck	3	—	—	—
	Common Eider	22	12	—	2
	King Eider	1	4	*5*	—
	White-winged Scoter	*6,202*	1,346	446	602
	Surf Scoter	375	*2,668*	183	449
	Common Scoter	*13,723*	6,348	363	576
	Ruddy Duck	1,586	2,398	*4,866*	2,876
	Hooded Merganser	*209*	158	169	104
	Common Merganser	147	*837*	495	636
	Red-breasted Merganser	*860*	487	565	378
Birds of Prey	Turkey Vulture	183	*231*	163	143
	Goshawk	2	4	4	5
	Sharp-shinned Hawk	6	*18*	16	10
	Cooper's Hawk	5	*14*	3	5
	Red-tailed Hawk	255	*392*	291	272
	Red-shouldered Hawk	28	*37*	19	22
	Swainson's Hawk	—	—	1	—
	Rough-legged Hawk	43	*85*	76	33
	Golden Eagle	—	1	2	2
	Bald Eagle	4	4	*6*	4
	Marsh Hawk	117	*230*	181	179
	Osprey	—	*1*	—	—
	Peregrine Falcon	*1*	1	—	1
	Pigeon Hawk	5	5	2	4
	Sparrow Hawk	454	597	688	437
Grouse	Ruffed Grouse	48	32	83	33
	Chukar	—	*1*	—	—

TABLE 10-3 (*Continued*)

GROUP	SPECIES	1969–70	1970–71	1971–72	1972–73
Pheasant & Quail	Bobwhite	606	517	419	507
	Ring-necked Pheasant	265	544	267	144
Turkey	Turkey	—	4	3	2
Rails	King Rail	—	2	1	—
	Clapper Rail	12	42	35	107
	Virginia Rail	23	14	11	2
	Sora	—	3	—	—
	Black Rail	—	1	—	—
	Common Gallinule	13	5	9	4
	American Coot	649	1,163	1,796	1,158
Shorebirds	Semipalmated Plover	1	2	1	3
	Piping Plover	—	—	3	—
	Killdeer	205	231	473	280
	Black-bellied Plover	244	377	669	174
	Ruddy Turnstone	47	67	132	134
	American Woodcock	13	46	42	22
	Common Snipe	86	129	94	97
	Willet	3	5	4	2
	Greater Yellowlegs	43	39	47	15
	Lesser Yellowlegs	1	7	26	7
	Knot	95	7	25	—
	Purple Sandpiper	75	304	173	349
	Least Sandpiper	—	6	2	15
	Dunlin	9,184	16,228	27,317	21,459
	Short-billed Dowitcher	—	3	2	5
	Semipalmated Sandpiper	183	106	65	102
	Western Sandpiper	5	154	16	31
	Spotted Sandpiper	1	—	—	—
	Marbled Godwit	—	—	—	3
	Sanderling	651	2,249	3,497	1,260
Gulls & Terns	Glaucous Gull	10	3	1	—
	Iceland Gull	8	4	4	2
	Great Black-backed Gull	5,154	5,759	4,434	3,161
	Lesser Black-backed Gull	1	—	—	—

TABLE 10-3 (*Continued*)

GROUP	SPECIES	1969–70	1970–71	1971–72	1972–73
	Herring Gull	48,921	72,398	55,771	43,547
	Ring-billed Gull	3,101	3,892	5,086	2,984
	Black-headed Gull	–	1	–	–
	Laughing Gull	12	14	30	14
	Bonaparte's Gull	5,618	2,794	1,782	2,122
	Little Gull	–	1	–	–
	Black-legged Kittiwake	–	12	2	1
	Forster's Tern	3	–	1	–
	Caspian Tern	–	–	1	–
	Black Tern	1	–	–	–
Auks	Razorbill	–	2	1	–
	Thick-billed Murre	–	–	1	–
	Dovekie	–	–	–	1
Dove	Mourning Dove	8,666	12,127	11,841	11,253
Parrot	Monk Parakeet	–	–	3	5
Owls	Barn Owl	2	9	8	8
	Screech Owl	54	66	36	32
	Great Horned Owl	23	119	62	39
	Barred Owl	2	1	2	1
	Long-eared Owl	13	19	24	15
	Short-eared Owl	18	36	14	18
	Saw-whet Owl	9	6	6	1
Kingfisher	Belted Kingfisher	77	125	179	140
Woodpeckers	Yellow-shafted Flicker	269	274	371	260
	Pileated Woodpecker	20	23	13	15
	Red-bellied Woodpecker	57	96	71	78
	Red-headed Woodpecker	–	2	14	1
	Yellow-bellied Sapsucker	7	15	11	16
	Hairy Woodpecker	273	393	310	278
	Downy Woodpecker	1,349	1,697	1,535	1,181
Flycatchers	Western Kingbird	–	–	3	–
	Eastern Phoebe	2	3	4	2

TABLE 10-3 (*Continued*)

GROUP	SPECIES	1969–70	1970–71	1971–72	1972–73
Lark	Horned Lark	2,474	2,110	1,185	1,161
Swallow	Tree Swallow	89	176	748	84
Crows	Blue Jay	3,064	7,945	7,723	3,698
	Common Crow	9,339	92,163	8,100	13,729
	Fish Crow	626	543	1,082	547
Titmice	Black-capped Chickadee	2,606	2,580	2,900	1,787
	Carolina Chickadee	1,322	1,772	1,574	1,340
	Boreal Chickadee	8	—	—	—
	Tufted Titmouse	1,968	2,859	2,387	1,828
Nuthatches	White-breasted Nuthatch	743	1,181	1,018	791
	Red-breasted Nuthatch	140	59	80	89
Creepers	Brown Creeper	112	208	208	116
Wrens	House Wren	1	1	1	2
	Winter Wren	25	35	41	28
	Carolina Wren	127	152	163	207
	Long-billed Marsh Wren	1	6	5	12
	Short-billed Marsh Wren	—	—	1	—
Mimics	Mockingbird	1,241	1,566	1,531	1,021
	Catbird	16	26	29	17
	Brown Thrasher	19	65	43	29
Thrushes	Robin	1,385	5,117	1,405	2,740
	Wood Thrush	—	—	1	—
	Hermit Thrush	43	47	35	40
	Swainson's Thrush	—	—	1	—
	Eastern Bluebird	52	23	33	45
Kinglets	Golden-crowned Kinglet	193	389	268	540
	Ruby-crowned Kinglet	57	49	339	59

TABLE 10-3 (*Continued*)

GROUP	SPECIES	*1969–70*	*1970–71*	*1971–72*	*1972–73*
Pipit	Water Pipit	51	*448*	32	10
Waxwing	Cedar Waxwing	97	*319*	297	249
Shrikes	Northern Shrike	—	1	2	3
	Loggerhead Shrike	2	*4*	2	3
Starling	Starling	71,851	68,723	*102,902*	69,474
Warblers	Black-and-white Warbler	—	—	*1*	1
	Tennessee Warbler	*1*	—	—	—
	Orange-crowned Warbler	—	*1*	—	1
	Nashville Warbler	*1*	—	—	—
	Myrtle Warbler	*1,892*	1,702	1,378	1,827
	Pine Warbler	3	*4*	3	—
	Prairie Warbler	*1*	—	—	—
	Palm Warbler	22	11	*30*	9
	Connecticut Warbler	—	—	—	*1*
	Yellowthroat	3	7	6	9
	Yellow-breasted Chat	1	1	*2*	—
	House Sparrow	12,839	16,670	*16,826*	9,748
	Eastern Meadowlark	911	*1,506*	813	657
Blackbirds & Orioles	Yellow-headed Blackbird	—	*1*	—	—
	Red-winged Blackbird	6,329	8,522	*22,180*	10,130
	Baltimore Oriole	8	7	*17*	3
	Bullock's Oriole	—	*1*	—	—
	Rusty Blackbird	271	*495*	272	213
	Boat-tailed Grackle	24	44	*118*	43
	Common Grackle	6,935	1,977	9,613	*11,474*
	Brown-headed Cowbird	3,320	2,580	*8,591*	3,502
Tanager	Western Tanager	—	*1*	—	—
Finches	Cardinal	2,564	*3,637*	2,383	2,379
	Dickcissel	9	5	1	1
	Black-headed Grosbeak	—	—	1	1

TABLE 10-3 (*Continued*)

GROUP	SPECIES	*1969–70*	*1970–71*	*1971–72*	*1972–73*
Finches	Evening Grosbeak	3,370	153	2,804	1,724
(cont'd.)	Purple Finch	360	161	405	*994*
	House Finch	1,522	*2,349*	1,944	1,693
	Pine Grosbeak	–	–	3	*41*
	Common Redpoll	*184*	3	152	1
	Pine Siskin	*2,782*	62	744	104
	American Goldfinch	*4,639*	1,530	3,515	3,772
	Red Crossbill	*220*	–	19	19
	White-winged Crossbill	1	1	3	–
	Rufous-sided Towhee	234	*552*	327	89
	Ipswich Sparrow	*47*	23	42	40
	Savannah Sparrow	160	342	*489*	157
	Grasshopper Sparrow	–	–	*1*	–
	Sharp-tailed Sparrow	8	42	21	*106*
	Seaside Sparrow	25	17	26	37
	Vesper Sparrow	14	*110*	14	7
	Lark Sparrow	*1*	–	1	–
	State-colored Junco	9,973	*11,939*	9,879	7,228
	Oregon Junco	2	3	–	2
	Tree Sparrow	*7,549*	4,712	4,593	3,181
	Chipping Sparrow	55	47	*254*	30
	Field Sparrow	*1,149*	1,090	901	729
	White-crowned Sparrow	164	103	*205*	12
	White-throated Sparrow	5,364	*6,711*	5,872	4,381
	Fox Sparrow	*416*	177	237	101
	Lincoln's Sparrow	–	*1*	–	–
	Swamp Sparrow	237	*362*	308	234
	Song Sparrow	3,880	4,719	4,054	2,197
	Lapland Longspur	*35*	11	17	24
	Snow Bunting	867	536	143	89

Part 2. *Big Day Counts.* There is usually one day each spring when bird watchers try to see as many species of birds as possible within a given area such as New Jersey.

To do this one must literally be in the field from dawn to dusk and cover a wide range of habitats, from inland forests to coastal marshes. In New Jersey, a mid-May survey yields the most species. Small groups of friends usually form the teams for such counts.

The typical census day begins well before dawn, often at a woodland swamp. Team members listen for nocturnal birds in the early morning darkness and tape-recorded calls sometimes evoke the response of a nearby Screech Owl or Barred Owl. By dawn a real chorus arises and species are added rapidly—merely hearing a bird counts as long as it is positively identified. The Swamp Sparrow and Eastern Wood Pewee are some of a dozen species that may be recorded before the sun's rays break the horizon. At sunrise many marsh birds are immediately obvious, including the Red-winged Blackbird, Yellowthroat, and Green Heron. Other birds may be elusive and require patience, such as the Sora Rail, Common Gallinule, or American Bittern. Since time is critical on a "big day," the census at the swamp is usually completed within an hour.

A deciduous forest is another essential habitat for the count, and it is best taken before mid-morning. In May the woodlands literally swarm with migrants on their way to northern breeding grounds. The forty or more species added here include several thrushes and many smaller songbirds. In fact, a team's success is often dependent on a knowledge of warbler songs for this morning period. Any species missed in the forest are not likely to be recorded in other habitats so it is imperative to make a thorough count. A team should strain to identify every possible bird, from a vireo in the top of a tall oak to a cuckoo calling in the distance. Usually everyone in the party tries to identify each species that is added to the list. Spotting scarce species is largely a matter of luck: the White-crowned Sparrow, House Finch, and Ruffed Grouse are examples of unpredictable birds. Such rare species add to the adventure of the day.

The last half of the morning is devoted to abandoned fields and farmyards. The most common birds include the Meadowlark, Sparrow Hawk, Field Sparrow, and Pheasant. Other possible finds in the fields are the Grasshopper Sparrow, Bobolink, and Upland Plover. Farmyard additions may include the Cowbird and Cliff Swallow. It is often essential to visit several fields of different ages to list all of the thirty species desired from this habitat.

The team travels next to the coast, pausing briefly for lunch in the pine barrens where several important species can be easily added—the Pine and Prairie warblers, and the Carolina Chickadee. Calling Bobwhites and Carolina Wrens may be heard.

The team's list should exceed one hundred species by the time it arrives at the shore, and the birds identified there will raise the final total of the count. Intense coverage should be made of a mud flat at low tide for an optimal variety of migrant shorebirds and of the adjacent marsh grass for Seaside and Sharp-tailed Sparrows, as well as Clapper Rails. Many species of terns, gulls, and egrets may be added as they fly by. Tidal pools or ponds should provide a variety of ducks and several "bonus" species, including the Yellow-crowned Night Heron and Louisiana Heron.

As sunset approaches the team usually heads to the ocean front for beach birds, including the Sanderling and Roseate Tern. Additional species should fly past the beach in migration lines—Common Loons and Double-crested Cormorants. Most of the ocean species are narrowly restricted to their habitat. After sunset the exhausted team returns home, pausing briefly to listen for Whip-poor-wills and a few final night birds. The cumulative list for the day will probably exceed 130 species.

SAMPLE "BIG DAY"

Below is an actual "big day" count from New Jersey that I made with Roger Meservey and Edward Murray on May 16, 1972. Our twelve-hour route included the Princeton Wildlife Refuge and Brigantine National Wildlife Refuge. The day was cool and we recorded 131 birds presented here in the standard checklist order.

Grebe	Pied-billed Grebe	Rails	Clapper Rail
Herons &	Great Blue Heron		American Coot
Egrets	Green Heron		American
	Little Blue Heron		Oystercatcher
	Cattle Egret	Shorebirds	Semipalmated Plover
	Common Egret		Piping Plover
	Snowy Egret		Killdeer
	Louisiana Heron		Black-bellied Plover
	Black-crowned Night		Ruddy Turnstone
	Heron		Whimbrel
	Glossy Ibis		Spotted Sandpiper
			Willet
Waterfowl	Mute Swan		Greater Yellowlegs
	Canada Goose		Knot
	Brant		Least Sandpiper
	Mallard		Dunlin
	Black Duck		Short-billed
	Gadwall		Dowitcher
	Blue-winged Teal		Semipalmated
	Wood Duck		Sandpiper
	Bufflehead		Sanderling
Birds of Prey	Turkey Vulture	Gulls & Terns	Great Black-backed
	Osprey		Gull
			Herring Gull
Quail &	Bobwhite		Ring-billed Gull
Pheasant	Ring-necked Pheasant		Laughing Gull

Gulls & Terns (cont'd.)	Forster's Tern Common Tern Least Tern Black Skimmer	Wrens	House Wren Long-billed Marsh Wren
Doves	Rock Dove Mourning Dove	Mimics	Mockingbird Catbird Brown Thrasher
Cuckoo	Yellow-billed Cuckoo	Thrushes	Robin Wood Thrush
Nighthawk	Common Nighthawk		Swainson's Thrush
Swift	Chimney Swift		Veery
Woodpeckers	Yellow-shafted Flicker	Waxwing	Cedar Waxwing
	Red-bellied Woodpecker	Starling	Starling
	Downy Woodpecker	Vireos	Red-eyed Vireo Warbling Vireo
Flycatchers	Eastern Kingbird Great-crested Flycatcher Eastern Phoebe Least Flycatcher Eastern Wood Pewee	Warblers	Black-and-white Warbler Prothonotary Warbler Blue-winged Warbler Tennessee Warbler Nashville Warbler Parula Warbler
Swallows	Tree Swallow Bank Swallow Rough-winged Swallow Barn Swallow Purple Martin		Yellow Warbler Magnolia Warbler Cape May Warbler Black-throated Blue Warbler Myrtle Warbler
Crows & Jay	Blue Jay Common Crow Fish Crow		Black-throated Green Warbler Chestnut-sided Warbler
Chickadees	Black-capped Chickadee Carolina Chickadee Tufted Titmouse		Blackpoll Warbler Pine Warbler Prairie Warbler Ovenbird Northern
Nuthatch	White-breasted Nuthatch		Waterthrush Yellowthroat

		Finches	Cardinal
	Canada Warbler		Rose-breasted
	American Redstart		Grosbeak
House	House Sparrow		Indigo Bunting
Sparrow			Purple Finch
			House Finch
Blackbirds	Bobolink		American Goldfinch
	Eastern Meadowlark		Rufous-sided Towhee
	Redwing Blackbird		Sharp-tailed Sparrow
	Orchard Oriole		Seaside Sparrow
	Baltimore Oriole		Vesper Sparrow
	Common Grackle		Chipping Sparrow
	Brown-headed		Field Sparrow
	Cowbird		Swamp Sparrow
Tanager	Scarlet Tanager		Song Sparrow

A history of "big day" censuses in the State by Edwin Stearns appeared in *Birding* magazine in the January and March issues of 1971. According to him, Charles Urner is essentially the originator of such spring counts in New Jersey, starting with a party list of 162 species in 1930. The party list grew under Urner to a maximum of 173 species in 1933, with an individual list of 163 species. These records remained unbroken until May 16, 1953, when a large party from the Urner Club tallied 175 species in New Jersey. A member of that party, Edwin Stearns, has gone on to become State champion with two counts of 176 species for his individual list (May 13, 1956, and May 16, 1959). The maximum for a single party is now 186 species, as set in eastern New Jersey on May 12, 1957. Stearns did an interesting tabulation of the "big day" records over a 20-year period and found a mid-May total of 239 species, but concluded that 160 species constituted a good record for any given year. For beginners in this sport I suggest the more reasonable goal of 100 species on the first New Jersey "big day." This should be challenge enough.

While May certainly provides maximum counts I have found it possible to have a "century day" (that is, to record more than a hundred species) throughout all the summer months.

The American Birding Association has started formal "big day" reports, and I conducted its first New Jersey count with 127 species (May 11, 1972). Others have now raised the "big day" record for the State to 172 species and there is no doubt a new total will soon succeed this 1973 report. Future possibilities are also suggested by the activities of the Delaware Valley Ornithological Club on the "big day" round-ups. This one-day count includes as many as sixty observers in a dozen parties in four states (Pennsylvania, New Jersey, Delaware, and Maryland). The club record is 248 species (May 10, 1970) with a remarkable single party record of 208 species in three states.

APPENDIX I

An Annotated Checklist of All Birds Known to Have Been Recorded in the State of New Jersey

The following list is a complete presentation of the 410 species recorded in New Jersey as of January 1, 1974. A few names are modified slightly from those given in most field guides. These modifications, listed below, were recently announced by the American Ornithologists' Union and will be widely adopted in the future. I indicate the field guide names (former names), followed by the proposed new names: Fulmar = Northern Fulmar, Leach's Petrel = Leach's Storm-Petrel, Wilson's Petrel = Wilson's Storm-Petrel, Common Egret = Great Egret, Wood Ibis = Wood Stork, Pintail = Northern Pintail, Shoveller = Northern Shoveller, American Widgeon = American Wigeon, Common Scoter = Black Scoter, Goshawk = Northern Goshawk, Marsh Hawk = Northern Harrier, Pigeon Hawk = Merlin, Sparrow Hawk = American Kestrel, Woodcock = American Woodcock, Upland Plover = Upland Sandpiper, Knot = Red Knot, Screech Owl = Northern Screech Owl, Mockingbird = Northern Mockingbird, Catbird = Gray Catbird, Parula Warbler = Northern Parula, and Yellowthroat = Common Yellowthroat.

A few birds that formerly were considered species will be treated as subspecies, as established by the union. These changes are repeated in the list itself for clarity. The Snow Goose now includes the former "Blue Goose," the Green-winged Teal includes "Common Teal," the Common Flicker includes both the "Yellow-shafted" and "Red-shafted Flicker," the Yellow-rumped Warbler includes both the "Myrtle Warbler" and "Audubon's Warbler," the Northern Oriole includes both the "Baltimore Oriole" and "Bullock's Oriole," the Savannah Sparrow includes the "Ipswich Sparrow," and the Dark-eyed Junco includes both the "Slate-colored Junco" and "Oregon Junco." I have included the quoted subspecies because they are still illustrated in all field guides and recognized by field workers.

Finally, the Traill's Flycatcher will be changed in the future to two species, reflected by song types: the Willow Flycatcher ("fitz-bew" song) and the Alder Flycatcher ("fee-bee-o" song). Both of these species occur in New Jersey.

GROUP	SPECIES
Loons	Common Loon—common migrant and winter visitor
	Red-throated Loon—common migrant and winter visitor; coastal
Grebes	Red-necked Grebe—rare in winter and as a migrant
	Horned Grebe—common winter resident
	Eared Grebe—very rare coastal visitor in winter
	Western Grebe—accidental visitor to coast from west
	Pied-billed Grebe—permanent resident; breeds
Albatross	Black-browed Albatross—accidental visitor to ocean in summer
Shearwaters	Sooty Shearwater—oceanic visitor in summer
	Manx Shearwater—oceanic visitor in summer; accidental
	Audubon's Shearwater—very rare oceanic visitor in summer
	Greater Shearwater—oceanic visitor in summer
	Cory's Shearwater—oceanic visitor in late summer and fall
Storm-Petrels	Leach's Storm-Petrel—rare oceanic visitor in late summer

GROUP	SPECIES

Wilson's Storm-Petrel—oceanic visitor in summer
White-faced Storm-Petrel—accidental oceanic visitor in summer

Fulmar
Northern Fulmar—oceanic visitor in winter; rare

Pelicans
American White Pelican—accidental visitor from west
Brown Pelican—accidental visitor from south

Gannets
Northern Gannet—winter visitor and common migrant; oceanic
Brown Booby—accidental visitor from south; oceanic

Cormorants
Great Cormorant—winter visitor on the coast
Double-crested Cormorant—common migrant; few in winter and summer
Anhinga—accidental visitor from the south

Frigatebird
Magnificent Frigatebird—accidental on the coast from the south

Herons
Great Blue Heron—common resident; breeds locally
Cattle Egret—summer resident; breeds in southern New Jersey
Great Egret—summer resident; breeds in southern New Jersey
Snowy Egret—summer resident; breeds in southern New Jersey
Louisiana Heron—uncommon in summer; breeds in southern New Jersey
Little Blue Heron—summer resident; breeds in southern New Jersey
Green Heron—common summer resident; breeds
Black-crowned Night Heron—permanent resident; breeds
Yellow-crowned Night Heron—local summer resident in southern New Jersey; breeds

Bitterns
Least Bittern—local summer resident throughout; breeds
American Bittern—summer and fall resident; breeds

GROUP	SPECIES
Stork	Wood Stork—accidental visitor from south
Ibis	Glossy Ibis—summer resident; breeds on coast
	White Ibis—summer visitor; very rare
Flamingo	American Flamingo—accidental visitor from south
Swans	Mute Swan—permanent resident; breeds. Introduced
	Whistling Swan—uncommon migrant and winter visitor
Geese	Canada Goose—common resident; breeds
	Brant—coastal resident in winter and migrant
	Black Brant—accidental visitor from west
	White-fronted Goose—very rare visitor from west
	Snow Goose—winter resident
	Ross' Goose—accidental visitor from west
	"Blue Goose"—rare migrant and winter resident (Subspecies of Snow Goose)
Ducks	Shelduck—accidental visitor from Europe
	Mallard—common nesting resident
	Black Duck—common nesting resident
	Gadwall—resident; rare breeder
	Northern Pintail—migrant; some in winter
	"Common Teal"—very rare visitor; winter (Subspecies of Green-winged Teal)
	Green-winged Teal—migrant; some in winter and resident
	Blue-winged Teal—migrant; some resident
	European Wigeon—rare winter visitor
	American Wigeon—migrant and winter visitor
	Northern Shoveller—resident; scarce breeder in summer
	Wood Duck—spring and summer resident; breeds; few in winter
	Fulvous Tree Duck—accidental visitor from the south
	Redhead—winter visitor and uncommon migrant
	Ring-necked Duck—migrant and winter visitor
	Tufted Duck—very rare visitor from Europe

GROUP   SPECIES

Canvasback—winter visitor
Greater Scaup—common winter visitor and migrant
Lesser Scaup—winter visitor and common migrant
American Goldeneye—common winter visitor
Barrow's Goldeneye—very rare winter visitor on coast
Bufflehead—common winter visitor
Oldsquaw—common winter visitor
Harlequin Duck—very rare winter visitor on coast
Common Eider—very rare winter visitor on coast
King Eider—rare winter visitor on coast
White-winged Scoter—common migrant and winter visitor on coast
Surf Scoter—common migrant and winter visitor on coast
Black Scoter—common migrant and winter visitor on coast
Ruddy Duck—resident but rare in summer; breeds
Hooded Merganser—migrant and winter visitor; few breed
American Merganser—winter visitor and common migrant
Red-breasted Merganser—winter visitor on coast

Vultures   Turkey Vulture—breeding resident
                Black Vulture—very rare visitor from the south

Kites   Swallow-tailed Kite—accidental visitor from the south
                Mississippi Kite—accidental visitor from the south

Hawks   Northern Goshawk—rare fall migrant and winter visitor
                Sharp-shinned Hawk—fall migrant and rare winter resident; has bred
                Cooper's Hawk—fall migrant and rare winter resident; has bred
                Red-tailed Hawk—resident and common migrant; breeds
                Red-shouldered Hawk—uncommon nesting resident; common migrant

GROUP	SPECIES
Hawks (cont'd.)	Broad-winged Hawk—summer nester and common fall migrant
	Swainson's Hawk—accidental migrant from the west
	Rough-legged Hawk—winter visitor
	Golden Eagle—rare migrant and winter visitor
	Bald Eagle—very rare resident; former nester; regular migrant
	Northern Harrier—migrant and uncommon breeding resident; few winter
Osprey	Osprey—uncommon resident spring through fall; breeds
Falcons	Gyrfalcon—accidental winter visitor from the north
	Peregrine Falcon—rare migrant and winter resident; has bred
	Merlin—migrant and rare winter resident
	American Kestrel—common breeding resident
	European Kestrel—accidental visitor from Europe
Grouse	Ruffed Grouse—breeding resident
	Heath Hen—former breeding resident in southern New Jersey; now extirpated
	Gray Partridge—unsuccessful introduction from Europe; extirpated
	Bobwhite—breeding resident in southern New Jersey
	Ring-necked Pheasant—common breeding resident; introduced
	Chukar—rare; introduced from the west
Turkey	Turkey—very rare resident in northern New Jersey
Crane	Sandhill Crane—accidental migrant from the west
Rails	King Rail—rare breeding resident
	Clapper Rail—common breeding resident, rare in winter; coastal
	Virginia Rail—breeding resident; rare in winter
	Sora—uncommon breeder in summer; migrant; few in winter

GROUP	SPECIES
	Yellow Rail—very rare migrant
	Black Rail—very rare summer resident at coast; breeds
	Corn Crake—accidental visitor from Europe
Gallinules	Purple Gallinule—accidental visitor from the south
	Common Gallinule—summer breeder; rare in winter
	American Coot—common resident except in summer; some breed
Oyster-catchers	American Oystercatcher—local breeding resident in summer; southern New Jersey
	Black Oystercatcher—accidental visitor from the west
Lapwing	European Lapwing—accidental visitor to coast from Europe
Plovers	Semipalmated Plover—common migrant
	Piping Plover—migrant and uncommon summer breeder
	Wilson's Plover—very rare summer visitor; has bred
	Killdeer—nesting resident; less common in winter
	Ruddy Turnstone—common migrant on coast
	American Golden Plover—uncommon fall migrant
	Black-bellied Plover—common migrant; some all year
Woodcocks	European Woodcock—accidental visitor from Europe
	American Woodcock—resident and common migrant; spring breeder
Snipes	Common Snipe—migrant and winter resident
	Great Snipe—accidental visitor from Europe
Sandpipers	Long-billed Curlew—accidental visitor from the west
	Whimbrel—coastal migrant
	Eskimo Curlew—rare coastal migrant; now extinct
	Upland Sandpiper—rare summer resident; breeds
	Spotted Sandpiper—breeding resident in summer
	Solitary Sandpiper—migrant
	Spotted Redshank—accidental visitor from Europe
	Willet—common nesting resident in summer
	Greater Yellowlegs—migrant; few in winter

GROUP	SPECIES
Sandpipers (cont'd.)	Lesser Yellowlegs—migrant; few in winter
	Red Knot—spring migrant; few in winter; coastal
	Purple Sandpiper—uncommon winter visitor; coastal
	Pectoral Sandpiper—migrant
	White-rumped Sandpiper—uncommon migrant
	Baird's Sandpiper—rare migrant in fall
	Least Sandpiper—common migrant; present at other times of the year
	Curlew Sandpiper—very rare migrant on coast
	Dunlin—common migrant and winter resident
	Short-billed Dowitcher—common migrant
	Long-billed Dowitcher—uncommon migrant
	Stilt Sandpiper—fall migrant; scarce in spring
	Semipalmated Sandpiper—common migrant; present at other times of the year
	Western Sandpiper—fall migrant; scarce in spring
	Buff-breasted Sandpiper—rare fall migrant
	Marbled Godwit—rare fall migrant
	Bar-tailed Godwit—accidental visitor from Europe
	Hudsonian Godwit—rare fall migrant
	Black-tailed Godwit—accidental visitor from Europe
	Ruff—very rare visitor throughout year
	Sanderling—common migrant in winter; scarce in early summer
Avocet	American Avocet—rare spring, summer, and fall visitor
Stilt	Black-necked Stilt—very rare spring visitor
Phalaropes	Red Phalarope—migrant; oceanic, far offshore
	Wilson's Phalarope—uncommon migrant
	Northern Phalarope—oceanic migrant
Jaegers	Pomarine Jaeger—rare migrant; oceanic
	Parasitic Jaeger—oceanic migrant; some along coast
	Long-tailed Jaeger—very rare ocean migrant
	Skua—accidental oceanic visitor from the north
Gulls	Glaucous Gull—rare winter visitor
	Iceland Gull—rare winter visitor

GROUP	SPECIES
	Great Black-backed Gull—common resident but rare breeder
	Lesser Black-backed Gull—accidental visitor from Europe
	Herring Gull—common resident but rare breeder
	Ring-billed Gull—common resident; does not breed in region
	Black-headed Gull—rare visitor from Europe
	Laughing Gull—breeding summer resident
	Franklin's Gull—accidental visitor from the west
	Bonaparte's Gull—migrant and winter resident
	Sabine's Gull—accidental visitor from the west
	Little Gull—rare visitor on coast in spring
	Ivory Gull—accidental visitor from arctic
	Black-legged Kittiwake—winter visitor on coast; rare
Terns	Gull-billed Tern—rare summer resident; few breeding records
	Forster's Tern—nesting summer resident and fall migrant
	Common Tern—nesting summer resident
	Arctic Tern—accidental migrant from the Atlantic
	Roseate Tern—very rare breeder in summer
	Sooty Tern—accidental visitor from the south
	Bridled Tern—accidental visitor from the south
	Noddy Tern—accidental visitor from the south
	Least Tern—summer resident; breeds
	Royal Tern—summer and fall visitor from the south
	Sandwich Tern—accidental visitor from the south
	Caspian Tern—rare migrant
	Black Tern—fall migrant
Skimmer	Black Skimmer—breeding summer resident
Auks	Razorbill—rare winter visitor on coast
	Common Murre—very rare winter visitor
	Thick-billed Murre—rare winter visitor
	Dovekie—rare winter visitor

GROUP	SPECIES
Auks (cont'd.)	Black Guillemot—very rare winter visitor Common Puffin—very rare winter visitor
Doves	Rock Dove (Pigeon)—common resident; breeds in every month Mourning Dove—common resident; long breeding season Passenger Pigeon—extinct in New Jersey before 1900 Ground Dove—accidental visitor from the south
Cuckoos	Yellow-billed Cuckoo—breeding resident in summer Black-billed Cuckoo—breeding resident in summer Smooth-billed Ani—accidental visitor from the south
Owls	Barn Owl—resident; breeds Northern Screech Owl—common breeding resident Great Horned Owl—resident; breeds in last half of winter Snowy Owl—rare winter visitor Hawk Owl—accidental visitor from the north Barred Owl—uncommon resident; breeds Long-eared Owl—rare breeding resident; most common in winter Short-eared Owl—scarce breeding resident; chiefly in winter Boreal Owl—accidental visitor from the north Saw-whet Owl—scarce winter visitor; rare breeder
Nighthawks	Chuck-will's-widow—rare summer resident in southern New Jersey; breeds Whip-poor-will—common summer breeder Common Nighthawk—common summer breeder
Swift	Chimney Swift—common summer breeder and migrant
Humming-bird	Ruby-throated Hummingbird—breeder and common migrant
Parrots	Carolina Parakeet—extinct in New Jersey since the nineteenth century Monk Parakeet—recent introduction; breeding

GROUP	SPECIES
Kingfisher	Belted Kingfisher—summer resident; rare in winter

Wood-
peckers
"Yellow-shafted" Flicker—common breeder; scarce in winter (Subspecies of Common Flicker)
"Red-shafted Flicker"—accidental western visitor (Subspecies of Common Flicker)
Pileated Woodpecker—uncommon breeder in northern New Jersey
Red-bellied Woodpecker—becoming common; breeding resident
Red-headed Woodpecker—rare resident; few breeding in northwestern New Jersey
Yellow-bellied Sapsucker—fall migrant and rare winter resident
Hairy Woodpecker—permanent resident; breeds
Downy Woodpecker—common permanent resident; breeds
Red-cockaded Woodpecker—accidental visitor from the south
Black-backed Three-toed Woodpecker—very rare winter visitor

Flycatchers
Eastern Kingbird—common summer breeder
Gray Kingbird—accidental visitor from the south
Western Kingbird—rare fall migrant
Fork-tailed Flycatcher—accidental visitor from the south
Scissor-tailed Flycatcher—accidental visitor from the west
Kiskadee—accidental visitor from the tropics
Great Crested Flycatcher—common breeder in summer
Eastern Phoebe—nesting resident in summer; few winter
Say's Phoebe—accidental visitor from the west
Yellow-bellied Flycatcher—rare migrant
Acadian Flycatcher—rare breeding resident in summer
Willow Flycatcher—summer resident; breeds (Formerly called Traill's Flycatcher)

GROUP	SPECIES
Flycatchers (cont'd.)	Alder Flycatcher—transient; few breed
	Least Flycatcher—summer resident; breeds
	Eastern Wood Pewee—summer resident; breeds
	Olive-sided Flycatcher—rare migrant
Lark	Horned Lark—resident; breeds in spring; scarce in summer
Swallows	Tree Swallow—breeding resident; common in migration; scarce in winter
	Bank Swallow—breeds in summer; common migrant
	Rough-winged Swallow—breeds in summer; common migrant
	Barn Swallow—common summer resident; breeds
	Cliff Swallow—uncommon migrant and rare summer breeder
	Purple Martin—breeding summer resident
Crows	Blue Jay—permanent resident; most common in migration; breeds
	Black-billed Magpie—accidental visitor from the west
	Common Raven—very rare visitor in northwestern New Jersey
	Common Crow—common resident; breeds
	Fish Crow—resident at coast; breeds
Titmice	Black-capped Chickadee—resident but most common in winter; breeds
	Carolina Chickadee—common breeding resident in southern New Jersey
	Boreal Chickadee—rare winter visitor
	Tufted Titmouse—common breeding resident
Nuthatches	White-breasted Nuthatch—resident; breeds
	Red-breasted Nuthatch—irregular winter visitor; breeds locally in northern New Jersey
Creeper	Brown Creeper—mostly winter resident; some breeding in northern New Jersey

GROUP	SPECIES
Wrens	House Wren—common summer resident; breeds
	Winter Wren—migrant and uncommon winter resident; few breed
	Bewick's Wren—accidental visitor from the west
	Carolina Wren—breeding resident
	Long-billed Marsh Wren—summer and fall resident; breeds
	Short-billed Marsh Wren—rare summer breeder
Mimics	Northern Mockingbird—common resident in recent years; breeds
	Gray Catbird—common summer resident; breeds
	Brown Thrasher—common summer resident; breeds
	Sage Thrasher—accidental visitor from the west
Thrushes	Robin—very common summer resident; breeds; scarce in winter
	Varied Thrush—accidental visitor from the west
	Wood Thrush—common summer resident; breeds
	Hermit Thrush—common migrant; scarce in winter; few breed in northern New Jersey
	Swainson's Thrush—common migrant
	Gray-cheeked Thrush—migrant
	Veery—migrant, and summer breeder in northern New Jersey
	Eastern Bluebird—uncommon breeding resident; mostly northern New Jersey
	Wheatear—accidental visitor from Europe
Gnatcatcher	Blue-gray Gnatcatcher—summer resident; breeds
Kinglets	Golden-crowned Kinglet—migrant; most common in fall; few breed in northern New Jersey
	Ruby-crowned Kinglet—migrant; few in winter
Pipit	Water Pipit—migrant and uncommon in winter
Waxwings	Cedar Waxwing—erratic resident
	Bohemian Waxwing—accidental visitor from the west

GROUP	SPECIES
Shrikes	Northern Shrike—very rare winter visitor from the north Loggerhead Shrike—migrant and rare winter visitor
Starling	Starling—resident and numerous; breeds spring and summer
Vireos	White-eyed Vireo—breeding resident; summer and fall Bell's Vireo—accidental visitor from the west Yellow-throated Vireo—uncommon migrant and summer breeder Solitary Vireo—transient; a few breed in northern New Jersey Red-eyed Vireo—common summer resident; breeds Philadelphia Vireo—uncommon migrant; chiefly in fall Warbling Vireo—summer resident; breeds in northern New Jersey
Warblers	Black-and-White Warbler—common migrant; breeds Prothonotary Warbler—rare summer breeder Swainson's Warbler—very rare summer visitor in southern New Jersey Worm-eating Warbler—breeding summer resident Golden-winged Warbler—migrant; some breeding in northern New Jersey Blue-winged Warbler—common summer resident; breeds Tennessee Warbler—migrant Orange-crowned Warbler—rare migrant and in winter Nashville Warbler—migrant; few nest in northern New Jersey Virginia's Warbler—accidental visitor from the west Northern Parula Warbler—migrant; possibly breeds in northwestern New Jersey Yellow Warbler—common summer resident; breeds Magnolia Warbler—common migrant; rare breeder in northwestern New Jersey Cape May Warbler—migrant; uncommon in spring

Black-throated Blue Warbler—migrant; scarce breeder in northern New Jersey

Black-throated Gray Warbler—accidental from the west

"Myrtle Warbler"—very common migrant; common winter resident on coast (Subspecies of Yellow-rumped Warbler)

"Audubon's Warbler"—accidental visitor from the west (Subspecies of Yellow-rumped Warbler)

Black-throated Green Warbler—migrant; breeds in northern New Jersey

Townsend's Warbler—accidental visitor from the west

Cerulean Warbler—rare migrant; few breeding locations

Blackburnian Warbler—migrant; limited breeding in northern New Jersey

Yellow-throated Warbler—very rare summer resident and breeder

Chestnut-sided Warbler—migrant and breeding summer resident

Bay-breasted Warbler—migrant

Blackpoll Warbler—common migrant

Pine Warbler—common migrant and breeder in summer

Prairie Warbler—summer resident and breeder

Palm Warbler—migrant; scarce in winter

Ovenbird—common summer resident; breeds

Northern Water-thrush—migrant; breeds in northern New Jersey

Louisiana Water-thrush—migrant and breeds in a few localities

Kentucky Warbler—rare summer resident and breeder

Connecticut Warbler—rare migrant

Mourning Warbler—rare migrant

Common Yellowthroat—common nesting resident in summer; few in early winter

Yellow-breasted Chat—scarce summer breeder; few remain through early winter

GROUP	SPECIES

Warblers (cont'd.)
Hooded Warbler—uncommon migrant and breeder
Wilson's Warbler—migrant
Canada Warbler—migrant; breeds in northwestern New Jersey
American Redstart—common migrant; breeds

House Sparrow
House Sparrow—abundant resident; breeds spring and summer

Blackbirds & Orioles
Bobolink—fall migrant; scarce in spring and as summer breeder
Eastern Meadowlark—resident; most common in summer as breeder
Western Meadowlark—accidental visitor from the west
Yellow-headed Blackbird—accidental visitor from the west
Red-winged Blackbird—resident; breeds; less common in winter
Orchard Oriole—scarce breeding resident in summer
"Baltimore Oriole"—common summer resident; breeds (Subspecies of Northern Oriole)
"Bullock's Oriole"—accidental visitor from the west (Subspecies of Northern Oriole)
Rusty Blackbird—migrant and uncommon winter resident
Brewer's Blackbird—very rare winter visitor from the west
Boat-tailed Grackle—rare resident and breeder in southern New Jersey
Common Grackle—breeding resident; abundant in migration
Brown-headed Cowbird—breeding resident

Tanagers
Western Tanager—accidental visitor from the west
Scarlet Tanager—summer breeder and common migrant
Summer Tanager—rare visitor from the south; has bred

GROUP	SPECIES
Finches	

Cardinal—common breeding resident

Rose-breasted Grosbeak—nesting summer resident

Black-headed Grosbeak—accidental visitor from the west

Blue Grosbeak—rare summer breeder in southern New Jersey

Indigo Bunting—summer breeder

Painted Bunting—accidental visitor from the south

Dickcissel—fall migrant; rare at other seasons and as local breeder

Evening Grosbeak—erratic winter visitor

Purple Finch—winter visitor; rare summer breeder in northern New Jersey

House Finch—resident; breeds; introduced

Pine Grosbeak—rare winter visitor

European Goldfinch—introduced and extirpated

Common Redpoll—rare winter visitor

Hoary Redpoll—accidental visitor in winter from the north

Pine Siskin—migrant and erratic winter visitor

American Goldfinch—common resident; breeds

Red Crossbill—rare winter visitor

White-winged Crossbill—rare winter visitor

Green-tailed Towhee—accidental visitor from the west

Rufous-sided Towhee—common breeder in summer; scarce in winter

"Ipswich Sparrow"—rare coastal visitor in winter (Subspecies of Savannah Sparrow)

Savannah Sparrow—resident; more common as a migrant

Grasshopper Sparrow—rare summer breeder

Henslow's Sparrow—rare summer breeder

Le Conte's Sparrow—accidental visitor from the west

Sharp-tailed Sparrow—breeding resident in summer at shore

Seaside Sparrow—breeding resident in summer at shore

GROUP	SPECIES
Finches (cont'd.)	Lark Bunting—very rare straggler from the west
	Vesper Sparrow—uncommon resident; breeds
	Lark Sparrow—very rare fall migrant from the west
	Black-throated Sparrow—accidental visitor from the west
	Bachman's Sparrow—accidental visitor from the south
	"Slate-colored Junco"—common winter resident; breeds some in northern New Jersey (Subspecies of Dark-eyed Junco)
	"Oregon Junco"—rare winter visitor from the west (Subspecies of Dark-eyed Junco)
	Cassin's Sparrow—accidental visitor from the west
	Tree Sparrow—common winter resident
	Chipping Sparrow—common summer resident; breeds
	Clay-colored Sparrow—very rare fall migrant from the west
	Field Sparrow—summer resident; breeds
	Harris's Sparrow—accidental visitor from the west
	White-crowned Sparrow—uncommon winter resident; migrant
	Golden crowned Sparrow—accidental visitor from the west
	White-throated Sparrow—common winter resident; breeds occasionally in northern New Jersey
	Fox Sparrow—migrant; scarce in winter
	Lincoln's Sparrow—rare migrant
	Swamp Sparrow—migrant and summer breeder; few in winter
	Song Sparrow—common resident; breeds
	Lapland Longspur—rare winter visitor
	Snow Bunting—uncommon winter visitor

APPENDIX II

Accidental Birds in New Jersey—
Records from 1960 to 1974

The following records were compiled from the regional reports of the New Jersey Audubon Society, as published quarterly in its magazine, *New Jersey Nature News*. Both the observers and the regional editors should receive credit for this list. It is hoped that this compilation of records will be useful and of interest to the many residents of New Jersey who enjoy the study of birds. For most bird watchers, the accidentals, those birds that are really not expected to occur in the State, are the most exciting finds. Rare species (such as the Western Kingbird) are not included, because they are found regularly each year in New Jersey, although in small numbers. The State has had an abundance of records of accidentals because it has many field observers; bird-watching activity is intense in the Garden State. The result is an exciting list, with many outstanding records throughout each year. And the total number of birds found in New Jersey continues to grow with each "First State Record"; the list currently consists of about 413 species.

The records are presented with the data of occurrence, location, and observer(s) name(s) in parentheses. Often a given bird is studied by several persons, and then credit is usually given to the one who first made the discovery. The species are arranged in the standard checklist and field-guide order.

I have chosen to use the published records of the *New Jersey Nature News* as those officially published by the State society. This quarterly magazine is received by more bird watchers in New Jersey than any other regional bulletin, and it is far more complete in its reporting than others. (In 1975 the society changed the name of its publication to *New Jersey Audubon*.)

Western Grebe
  January 21, 1962—Cape May (M. Sheldrick)
  December 5, 1968—Centennial Lake (T. Rowley)
  February 22, 1970—Brigantine Refuge (J. Meritt)
Eared Grebe
  April 1965—Brigantine Refuge (F. Moody & H. Saxon)
  December 29, 1968—Cape May (A. Brady)

Black-browed Albatross
  October 7, 1974—Cape May (Axtell & Brady)
White-faced Storm Petrel
  September 5, 1973—off Avalon (T. Koebel)
Brown Pelican
  August 5, 1969—Normandy Beach (G. Woolfenden)
Anhinga
  September 25, 1971—Cape May (K. Berlin, *et al.*), *First State Record*
White-fronted Goose
  April 1961—Brigantine Refuge (S. Spatz & C. Ross)
  January 1967—Brigantine Refuge (H. Megargee)
  May 1967—Brigantine Refuge (W. Parker)
  April 16, 1972—Plainsboro (C. Rogers)
Ross' Goose
  April 1972—Brigantine Refuge (many observers). *First State Record*
Cinammon Teal
  September 1962—Brigantine Refuge (F. Welch). *First State Record*
  November 1974—Brigantine Refuge (J. Danzenbaker)
Fulvous Tree Duck
  October 1961—Brigantine Refuge (many observers). *First State Record*
  April 1965—Trenton Marsh (R. Blicharz)
  May 29, 1965—Cape May (A. Brady & E. Choate)
  May 26, 1966—Secaucus Marshes (A. Barber)
  Fall 1966—Brigantine Refuge (many observers)
  Fall 1974 (many observers)

Tufted Duck
>February 1966–Edgewater (many observers). *First State Record*
>Winter 1966–67–Edgewater (L. Bottone & F. Lohrer)
>December 30, 1967–Edgewater (A. Barber)
>February 1971–Point Pleasant (R. Chamberlain)

Swallow-tailed Kite
>September 20, 1970–Paterson (P. Del Vecchio)
>May 12, 1972–Cape May (F. McLaughlin)

Black Vulture
>March 18, 1961–Fort Mott (S. Hardy)
>Spring 1962–South Mountain Reservation (H. Armitt)
>March 7, 1964–Harlingen (R. Thorsell)
>May 1964–Cape May (J. Cadbury & I. Black)
>March 6, 1966–Blackwood (J. Meritt)
>November 4, 1968–Ridgewood (S. Bailey)
>May 1969–Frankford Township (D. Richards)
>April 22, 1970–Yard Creek (M. Wolfarth)
>Fall 1970–Cape May (E. Choate, *et al.*)
>May 28, 1972–Hainesburg (J. Taylor)
>June 2, 1973–Stokes Forest (W. Sandford)

Swainson's Hawk
>October 23, 1971–New Vernon (A. Kome). *Second State Record*
>September 16, 1973–Cape May (W. Clark)

Gyrfalcon
>October 27, 1969–Racoon Ridge (T. Koebel)
>Winter 1971–72–Brigantine Refuge (many observers)

European Kestrel
>September 23, 1972–Cape May (W. Clark) *First State Record*

White Ibis
>May 26, 1965–Brigantine Refuge (M. Luker & W. Cullman)
>May 30, 1965–Cape May (E. Litchfield, *et al.*)
>July 1, 1966–Stone Harbor (many observers)
>August 1968–Cape May (many observers)
>July 27, 1972–Oceanville (J. Stasz)

American Flamingo
>August 1964–Brigantine Refuge (many observers). *First State Record*

Sandhill Crane
>April 1969–Troy Meadows (R. McKenzie & J. McManus)
>1969–70–Yellow Frame (G. Johnson, *et al.*)
>April 5, 1970–Brigantine Refuge (J. Meritt)

March 15, 1971—Stillwater (many observers)

August 21, 1972—Troy Meadows (G. Mahler & H. Wallum)

Purple Gallinule

May 1964—Great Swamp (many observers)

June 6, 1964—Brigantine Refuge (many observers)

June 17, 1972—Avon (G. Bodeep)

April 1973—Eatontown (W. Sandford)

Summer 1974—Monmouth Co. (many observers). Several records

Black-necked Stilt

August 1966—Stone Harbor (M. Brocklebank, *et al.*)

April 28, 1972—Brigantine Refuge (Deemer)

April 28, 1973—Cape May (K. Seager)

Bar-tailed Godwit

Summer 1971—Brigantine Refuge (many observers)

May 1972—Somer's Point (R. Rosche)

May 1973—Longport (many observers)

Summer 1974—Brigantine Refuge (many observers)

Black-tailed Godwit

Summer 1971—Brigantine Refuge (many observers). *First State Record*

Spotted Redshank

May 1965—Brigantine Refuge (several observers). *First State Record*

August 18, 1972—Manahawkin (F. Lesser)

Great Snipe

September 1963—Cape May (many observers). *First State Record*

Lesser Black-backed Gull

December 1962—North Arlington (M. Wolfarth)

January 1972—Jersey City (R. Ryan)

December 1974—Jersey City (Toffic & Wallum)

December 31, 1974—Belmar (P. W. Smith)

Skua

June 14, 1969—Avalon (Reimen). *First State Record*

Sandwich Tern

September 26, 1968—Tuckerton (E. Choate, *et al.*)

May 15, 1969—Cape May (E. Choate, *et al.*)

April 16, 1972—North Cape May (K. Seager)

Sooty Tern

Summer 1960 Hurricane—Cape May & Island Beach (many observers). Several recorded

June 23, 1972—Cape May (F. McLaughlin)

September 3, 1972—Long Branch (R. Smith)

Bridled Tern

Summer 1960 Hurricane—Island Beach State Park (B. Grant). Several recorded.

September 4, 1966—Brigantine Refuge (R. Chamberlain & R. Grant)

Noddy Tern

Summer 1960 Hurricane—Stone Harbor & Island Beach State Park (many observers)

Ground Dove

Winter 1961–62—Brigantine Refuge (R. Leeds, *et al.*)

Boreal Owl

November 1962—Raritan Arsenal (J. Mish). *Second State Record*

Red-shafted Flicker

June 11, 1964—Brigantine Refuge (R. Leeds)

Scissor-tailed Flycatcher

September 7, 1966—Avalon (H. Mills)

Fork-tailed Flycatcher

August 23, 1968—Cape May (B. Murray)

September 4, 1972—Brigantine Refuge (J. Danzenbaker)

September 4, 1972—Cape May (F. & M. Bleiers)

Kiskadee Flycatcher

December 1960—Cape May (many observers). *First State Record*

Say's Phoebe

October 2, 1960—Brigantine Refuge (R. Leeds)

Black-billed Magpie

March 19, 1960—Englewood (R. Brinckerhoff)

May 19, 1965—Wildwood (Manica)

Bewick's Wren

October 13, 1962—Cape May (R. Benedict)

Varied Thrush

Winter 1965–66—Moorestown (A. Blomquist)

November 23, 1971—Tenafly (A. Fritts)

Wheatear

September 1970—Brigantine Refuge (R. Chamberlain)

October 1, 1974—Brigantine Refuge (many observers)

Bohemian Waxwing

February 3, 1962—Princeton (I. Talmi)

April 1962—Flemington (H. Drinkwater)

November 30, 1968—Barnegat Light (Litch)

Swainson's Warbler

May 1968—Lindwood (W. Savelle). *First State Record*

Townsend's Warbler

Winter 1971–72—Princeton (T. Poole, *et al.*). *First State Record*

Black-throated Gray Warbler
  September 29, 1962—Island Beach State Park (Operation Recovery)
  November 7, 1964—Franklin (many observers)
  November 16, 1969—Mountainside (C. Burk)
  Fall 1969—Island Beach State Park (Operation Recovery)
  September 13, 1974—Cape May (many observers)
Western Meadowlark
  July 4, 1961—Blawenburg (J. Meritt)
  June 30, 1964—Plainsboro (F. Loetcher)
  June 22, 1965—Sandtown (C. Reynard)
Yellow-headed Blackbird
  October 1960—Brigantine Refuge (W. Parker)
  April 1961—Upper Saddle River (T. Crockett)
  December 1963—Troy Meadows (R. Thorsell)
  November 12, 1964—South Amboy (B. Knorr)
  February 9, 1965—Wood Ridge (D. Pallas)
  September 30, 1965—Ship Bottom (H. Michaels)
  September 1966—Brigantine Refuge (many observers)
  December 26, 1966—Woodbury (T. Poole)
  January 10, 1967—Mickleton (J. Sjoberg)
  May 1968—Great Swamp (many observers)
  October 13, 1968—Dutch Neck (M. Doscher)
  May 17, 1970—Brigantine Refuge (R. Chamberlain)
  December 26, 1970—Bergen County Christmas Count
  November 14, 1972—Mickleton (C. Bresler)
  March 17, 1973—Hopewell (T. Bogia)
  April 5, 1974—Rutherford (E. Brown)
Brewer's Blackbird
  December 1960—Hampton Township, Sussex (I. Black)
  December 1960—Cape May (Delaware Valley Ornithological Club)
  December 21, 1965—Wenonah (W. Middleton)
  December 1970—Livingston (R. Worthing)
Bullock's Oriole
  December 1960—Cape May (M. Staffer, *et al.*)
  December 1964—Ridgewood (McEntee)
  September 25, 1966—Cape May (J. Yrizarry, *et al.*)
  October 7, 1969—Wood Ridge (D. Pallas)
  January 9, 1972—Piscataway (D. Walton)
Western Tanager
  September 1960—Fairlawn (D. Preston)

December 26, 1960—Maplewood (A. Bender)
March 31, 1962—Branchville (Valerio)
August 21, 1962—River Vale (G. Komorowski)
January 2, 1971—Brigantine Refuge (many observers)
December 30, 1972—Braddock's Mill (H. Spendelow)

Black-headed Grosbeak
February 5, 1960—Maplewood (E. Chamberlin)
December 1960—Cape May (Delaware Valley Ornithological Club)
October 4, 1962—Cape May (W. Russell)
January 28–30, 1965—Asbury Park (Wisner)
February 10, 1965—Wenonah (Schwartz)
December 1966—Franklin (L. Cherepy)
December 26, 1971—Woodbury (D. Hill)
December 17, 1972—Princeton (K. Bramwell)
December 1974—Rumson (many observers)

Green-tailed Towhee
January 1961—Newton (G. Johnson). *Second State Record*
December 9, 1962—Whitesville (D. Kunkle)

Black-throated Sparrow
Winter 1961–62—New Brunswick (W. MacKenzie, *et al.*). *First State Record*
December 1974—N. Arlington (many observers)

Brambling
April 1965—Branchville (many observers). *Second State Record*

Le Conte's Sparrow
May 1964—Jamesburg (M. Miskimen & J. Swinebroad)
October 12, 1968—Island Beach State Park (R. Blicharz)

Lark Bunting
May 26, 1962—Delaware Bay (C. Noden, *et al.*)

Harris' Sparrow
Spring 1966—Princeton (many observers). *Second State Record*
October 7, 1967—Island Beach (Operation Recovery)
September 21, 1968—Sparta (L. Edwards)
November 1968—Grover's Mill (M. Taylor)
December 26, 1971—Secaucus (R. Ryan)

Golden-crowned Sparrow
October 7, 1962—Cape May (many observers). *First State Record*

APPENDIX III

Aids to Bird-Watching in New Jersey

This appendix provides directions for developing interest in birds. Three short bibliographies provide the titles of twenty-four useful references for the home library, covering such topics as bird feeders, field identification, and bird biology. Popular magazines, checklists, and bird-song records for New Jersey field observers are listed also.

The bird and nature study clubs of the State are listed geographically for those who wish to take field trips and join in related group activities. Many clubs have active programs throughout the year.

Readers seeking new areas to explore can consult the section on bird-watching locations, which identifies most of the State's sanctuaries. Finally, there is a brief description of the ornithology collections in New Jersey.

GUIDES TO BIRDS AND BIRD-WATCHING

Arbib, Robert, *et al. Enjoying Birds Around New York City.* New York, 1966. A guide to good bird locations in the northeastern New Jersey and New York area that can be easily visited. Also a seasonal calendar of birds, instructions on bird houses, feeders, *et cetera.*

Barton, Roger. *How to Watch Birds.* New York, 1961. A good companion to the field guides. How to identify, make feeders, and take bird photographs. Also chapters on plantings for birds, binoculars, and record-keeping. A valuable contribution from the President Emeritus of the New Jersey Audubon Society.

Brady, Alan, *et al. A Field List of Birds of the Delaware Valley Region.* Delaware Valley Ornithological Club, Philadelphia, 1972. The most up-to-date regional calendar for birds. The monthly abundance of each species is reviewed with bar graphs. A great help to those interested in arrival and departure dates, as well as breeding periods.

Bull, John. *Birds of the New York Area.* New York, 1964. This is probably the most authoritative regional book available. It includes all of North Jersey, from Flemington and Point Pleasant to the New York border. The exhaustive text presents detailed information on the status of each species, abundance, breeding, and migration in the area. Written for the serious observer.

Fables, David. *Annotated List of New Jersey Birds.* Urner Club, Newark, 1955. A good species-by-species account of the distribution and abundance of each species in the State. Unfortunately it is now out of date (for example, forty more species have been added to the State's list since 1955).

Heintzelman, Donald. *The Hawks of New Jersey.* New Jersey State Museum Bulletin 13, Trenton, 1970. One hundred pages of informative introduction to these birds of prey. Well illustrated.

Heintzelman, Donald. *A Guide to Northeastern Hawk Watching.* Published privately, 1972. A small but useful paperback with specific directions on how and where to look for hawks. Included are New Jersey's major outlooks at Cape May Point, Montclair, Raccoon Ridge, and Sunrise Mountain.

Hickey, Joseph. *A Guide to Bird Watching.* New York, 1963. An excellent guide to bird counts, migration watching, bird banding, and the like. This is a meaty book for those who want to pursue the hobby beyond merely the identification of birds.

Pettingill, Olin S. *A Guide to Bird Finding.* New York, 1951. A useful directory of where to find birds, describing key parks and refuges, and so forth. Areas of New Jersey included are: Atlantic City, Boonton, Brigantine, Bound Brook, Bridgeton, Caldwell, Camden, Cape May, Chatham, Freehold–Point Pleasant, Manahawkin, Milford, Montclair, Newark, Newton, Princeton, Salem, Sussex, Trenton, and Tuckerton.

Peterson, Roger. *A Field Guide to the Birds.* Boston, 1947. A must for any person starting to learn birds. This book started the field-guide movement and introduced the hobby of bird-watching to thousands. Well illustrated for each species in eastern North America.

Pough, Richard. *Audubon Water Bird Guide* and *Audubon Land Bird Guide.* New York, 1951. These provide excellent illustrations with rich color plates. The two volumes are too much to carry into the field, but they provide good home reading on the habits and behavior of each species.

Robbins, Chandler, *et al. A Guide to Field Identification—Birds of North America.* New York, 1966. A highly recommended guide, with *all* species shown in color. This is probably the most popular field guide today.

Stone, Witmer. *The Birds of New Jersey.* Annual Report of the New Jersey State Museum, Trenton, 1908. Out of print. A detailed discussion of bird life at the turn of the century. Of real historic interest, showing the effects of former hunting practices and egg collecting.

Stone, Witmer. *Bird Studies at Old Cape May.* New York, 1965. Two volumes. This is an exact reprint of the 1937 work, which is out of print and quite expensive. It is the most thorough book on the birds of New Jersey, with much natural history included. Anyone interested in coastal species will be especially glad to own a copy of this paperback reprint.

BOOKS ON AVIAN BIOLOGY

Cruickshank, Alan and Helen. *1001 Questions Answered about Birds.* New York, 1958. A review of the biology of birds, their behavior, and conservation. A highly recommended popular book; inexpensive.

Griffin, Donald. *Bird Migration.* New York, 1964. A good account of the modern studies of migration.

Lanyon, Wesley. *Biology of Birds.* New York, 1963. An inexpensive paperback; interesting text.

Peterson, Roger. *The Birds.* New York, 1963. A popular introduction to the world of birds; heavily illustrated with fine color photographs. Informative and interesting.

Stefferud, Alfred, ed. *Birds in Our Lives.* U.S. Government Printing Office, Washington, D.C., 1966. A large volume that reviews birds from many aspects, such as sports, husbandry, as pests and pets, in literature, falconry, and conservation. A good summary at a reasonable price.

Welty, Joseph. *The Life of Birds.* New York, 1963. This is probably the most widely used ornithology text in colleges today. An up-to-date review of avian biology.

Wetmore, Alexander, *et al. Water, Prey and Game Birds* and *Song and Garden Birds.* Washington, D.C., 1964. A beautiful two-volume set with pictures of all North American birds. The text provides brief but excellent natural history, and the set includes two bird-song records.

BIRD BEHAVIOR

Armstrong, E. 1965. *Bird Display and Behavior.* (Dover Publications, N.Y.) An excellent review of courtship and nesting ceremonies, social displays, and territorial behavior of birds throughout the world. Illustrated with photographs and drawings.

Burtt, H. 1967. *The Psychology of Birds.* (Macmillan Co., N.Y.) A discussion of bird perceptions and motivations. Topics include instinctive behavior, migration, learning, social behavior, and communication. The popular text is quite readable.

Sparks, J. 1970. *Bird Behavior.* (Grosset & Dunlap, N.Y.) An elementary introduction to the many aspects of bird behavior. Color illustrations on each page well illustrate the principles of the text.

Tinbergen, N. 1967. *The Herring Gull's World.* (Doubleday &

Co., N.Y.) A quality reproduction of the classic original is available in this paperback edition. Tinbergen's pioneering studies show how ethologists literally learn the language of the birds. Well illustrated throughout.

Guides to Bird Nests, Houses, and Feeders

Arbib, Robert, and Tony Soper. *Hungry Bird Book.* New York, 1970. Descriptions of yard improvements that will attract a variety of birds.

"Attracting and Feeding Birds." Fish & Wildlife Service Conservation Bulletin No. 1, U.S. Government Printing Office, 1973. A short pamphlet on bird feeders and plants that are attractive to birds.

Headstrom, Richard. *A Complete Field Guide to Nests in the United States.* New York, 1970. The greater part of the book deals with the identification of bird nests.

"Homes for Birds." Fish and Wildlife Service Conservation Bulletin No. 14, U.S. Government Printing Office, 1969. A good booklet that accurately describes and shows how to construct houses for a wide variety of birds.

Popular Magazines on Field Ornithology

"American Birds." Published by the National Audubon Society, New York. This magazine presents seasonal reviews of the bird life in each area of the country; also yearly breeding-bird censuses and Christmas counts.

"New Jersey Nature News." Published by the New Jersey Audubon Society, 790 Ewing Avenue, Franklin Lakes, New Jersey. A great help for New Jersey residents—conservation and field trips of the local Audubon Society with good field notes each season.

Checklists

Numerous checklists are available for small areas in New Jersey; these are most easily obtained through local Audubon societies. A few examples are provided below.

"Annotated List of Birds of High Point State Park and Stokes
State Forest" by Dryden Kuser
"Birds of the Watchung" by the Union County Outdoor Educa-
tion Center
"Checklist of Birds of the Princeton Wildlife Refuge" by the
Princeton Open Space Commission
"Birds of Great Swamp National Wildlife Refuge" and "Birds
of Brigantine National Wildlife Refuge" by the U.S. Depart-
ment of the Interior (available at the refuges)

Complete regional (New Jersey) checklists are available on
inexpensive field cards that fit in the pocket. Two sources are
given here; commercial lists are sometimes available as advertised
in magazines.

"Daily Field Checklist of Birds of Eastern North America"—
Livingston Publishing Company, Box 162, Wynnewood, Pa.
19072
"Linnaean Field Cards"—Linnaean Society, American Museum
of Natural History, Central Park West at 79th Street, New
York, N.Y. 10024

Records

Many bird-song records are now available. The Cornell
Laboratory of Ornithology, 159 Sapsucker Woods Road, Ithaca,
New York 14850, the largest "natural sounds" laboratory in the
world, has a catalogue of its recordings.
Three of the most popular albums are:

"A Field Guide to Bird Songs"—Two 12″-records with the songs
and calls of more than three hundred species arranged in
field-guide order.
"American Bird Songs"—Two 12″-records that present a wide
variety of familiar species, arranged by habitats.
"An Evening in Sapsucker Woods"—an enjoyable 10″-disk that

follows the evening chorus of natural sounds in a woodland. The opposite side has the calls and songs uninterrupted by identifications.

BIRD AND NATURE CLUBS

Below are listed bird clubs and other organizations that conduct bird-watching field trips. Many of the groups have films or lectures and regularly guided trips. Specific information about these clubs may be obtained from the local phone book or through the New Jersey Audubon Society, 790 Ewing Avenue, Franklin Lakes, N.J. 07417. (This list is adapted from Austin Lentz and Albert Hetzell, *A Guide to Nature Study in New Jersey,* Rutgers University Co-operative Extension Service Leaflet 433-A, 1971.)

Audubon Wildlife Society, Audubon
Cape May Geographic Society, Cape May
Chatham Nature Club, Chatham
Fyke Nature Association, Ramsey
Gloucester County Nature Club, Wenonah
Hackensack Audubon Society, Hackensack
Haddonfield Nature Science Club, Haddonfield
Hunterdon County Bird Club, High Bridge
Long Beach Island Conservation Society, Barnegat Light
Monmouth Nature Club, Middletown
Montclair Bird Club, Montclair
Morris Plains Audubon Society, Morris Plains
Ocean Nature and Conservation Society, Lakewood
Palisades Nature Association, Englewood
Paterson Nature Club, Paterson
Pemberton Bird Club, Pemberton
Ridgewood Audubon Society, Ridgewood
Summit Nature Club, Summit
Sussex County Bird Club, Sparta
Sussex County Nature Study Club, Newton

Trenton Naturalist Club, Trenton
Urner Ornithological Club, Newark
Vineland Nature Club, Vineland
Watchung Nature Club, Plainfield
Westfield Bird Club, Cranford
Witmer Stone Club, Stone Harbor

Many of these clubs sponsor excellent Audubon Screen-Tours, full-color nature films, through the winter months. These are available to the public and usually advertised in local newspapers.

WHERE TO FIND BIRDS

Listed below are some of the best open areas in the State. Directions for reaching most of these locations are given in the book *Away We Go!* edited by Michaela M. Mole (New Brunswick, 1971). Other locations are easily found on standard road maps.

In the list those areas that have a nature trail or museum or other interpretive facility are marked with an asterisk. Many new areas of the State's "Green Acres" program are also becoming attractive to bird watchers.

Atlantic County
   Brigantine National Wildlife Refuge, Oceanville
Bergen County
   *Baldwin Wildlife Sanctuary, Mahwah
   *Campgaw Mountain Reservation, Mahwah
   *Wildlife Center, Wyckoff
   *Closter Nature Center, Closter
   *Palisades Greenbrook Sanctuary, Englewood
   *Hawes School Outdoor Laboratory, Glen Rock
   *Indian Hills Outdoor Laboratory, Franklin Lakes
   *Joyce Kilmer Natural Laboratory, Mahwah
   *Lucine L. Lorrimer Sanctuary, Franklin Lakes

Norwood Park, Norwood
Ridgewood Preserve, Ridgewood
*Tenafly Nature Center, Tenafly
Burlington County
*Stokes Woods Sanctuary, Moorestown
Camden County
*Cherry Hill Nature Trail Area, Cherry Hill
Cape May County
*Bennett Bog Wildlife Sanctuary, Erma
Cape May Point Preserve, Cape May Point
Stone Harbor Bird Sanctuary, Stone Harbor
Essex County
Eagle Rock Reservation, West Orange
South Mountain Reservation, South Orange
West Essex Park, Cedar Grove
*Cora Hartshorn Arboretum, Short Hills
Montclair Hawk Lookout, Montclair
Mountainside Park, Upper Montclair
Outdoor Education Center, Irvington
Hunterdon County
*Reading Tract, White House
Mercer County
Princeton Wildlife Refuge, Princeton
Herrontown Woods, Princeton
John A. Roebling Memorial Park, Trenton
Middlesex County
Johnson Park, Highland Park
*Frank Helyar Nature Trail, Cook College, New Brunswick
*Boy Scout Museum & Trail, North Brunswick
Monmouth County
*Holmdel Park, Holmdel
*Monmouth Museum Nature Trail, Holmdel
Morris County
*Great Swamp National Wildlife Refuge, Morristown
*Great Swamp Nature Center, Morristown
*Jefferson Reservation, Milton

*Lewis Morris Park, Morristown
*Morristown National Historic Park, Morristown
*Schiff Scout Reservation, Mendham
Troy Meadows, Parsippany-Troy Hills
Passaic County
   South Mountain, Paterson
Somerset County
   William L. Hutcheson Forest, Rutgers University, Middle-
     bush
   *Scherman Wildlife Sanctuary, Bernardsville
Union County
   *Trailside Museum and Science Center, Mountainside

In addition to these areas, New Jersey has a rich assortment of State parks and State forests. The locations and facilities of these public areas can be found on most road-maps. I have listed them here to increase awareness of the many areas to explore.

State Forests
   Abram S. Hewitt, Bass River, Belleplain, Double Trouble, Jenny Jump, Lebanon, Norvin Green, Penn, Stokes, Wharton, and Worthington.

State Parks
   Allaire, Barnegat Lighthouse, Bull's Island, Cheesequake, Edison, Fort Mott, Hacklebarney, High Point, Hopatcong, Island Beach, Musconetcong, Palisades, Parvin, Rancocas, Ringwood, Round Valley, Sandy Hook, Saxton Falls, Shepherd Lake, Spruce Run, Stephens, Swartswood, Tallman Mountain, Voorhees, Washington Crossing, Washington Rock, and Wawayanda.

COLLECTIONS OF BIRD SPECIMENS IN NEW JERSEY

The most outstanding museum collection of birds in New Jersey is in Guyot Hall at Princeton University. Under the curatorship of Charles H. Rogers the collection has become a model teaching set—with 15,000 specimens representing all but one of the families of birds of the world. It is rich in local birds and several distant regions (Thailand, India, Sikkim, and Europe). The pheasants and hummingbirds are especially well represented.

The next largest collection is also at a university, nearby Rutgers. Charles Leck is the curator of this collection at Nelson Laboratory on the Busch campus in New Brunswick. The collection, with 100 bird families, is used in teaching introductory ornithology and vertebrate zoology at Rutgers College.

The New Jersey State Museum at Trenton houses a collection of recent specimens, with emphasis on New Jersey and Mexico. Most of the skins have some field notes on the bird's natural history; some have been prepared by a modern "freeze-dried" method, yielding lifelike mounted birds.

Teaching collections are also at Fairleigh Dickinson University, Garden State Academy, Newark Museum, Paterson Museum, and Trenton State College.